THRIVING IN OUR TIMES

Also by Cathy Caswell

Logosynthesis: Enjoying Life More Fully

PRAISE FOR *THRIVING IN OUR TIMES*

By sharing both her personal story and professional development Cathy has gifted us with insight into an elegant response to complex, individual challenges. We owe it to ourselves and to those around us to examine Logosynthesis and how the proper use of three simple but powerful sentences can improve life for all concerned.

Blair Richards, MBA
CIO at Halifax Port ILA/HEA

Every day there is more compelling evidence for each of us to consider and to tap into our body's intelligence, because our brains do not work in a vacuum. All experience happens in our bodies. We learn to listen to the impact distress, change and increased chronic pressure has on our emotional and physical health or we work hard to discount it, avoid it and even pretend emotions don't affect us.

I was introduced to Logosynthesis by my therapist a number of years ago, at a time when I was experiencing burnout and in the throes of a personal crisis and extreme feelings of overwhelm. Cathy's story of her own journey using Logosynthesis, as well as her natural skill of breaking down and guiding understanding of how and why it works and how to integrate it into daily living during our new normal, is essential reading. This is a life-changing, healthy practice to help you gain skills to build resilience, to cope in the moment, and to deepen self-awareness with use. Don't wait.

Kim MacDonald, MBA
Founder - 13 FACTORS for Business Growth

Thriving
IN OUR TIMES

From reactions to action
using Logosynthesis®

CATHY CASWELL

Disclaimer: This book shares the author's experience of using the Logosynthesis model. The content is the author's personal perspective only and is provided only as general information to help others learn about Logosynthesis. The material presented is not meant as a substitute for medical treatment nor a promise to solve problems. The author accepts no responsibility or liability for misuse of the information contained in this book. Names and personal details have been changed in the examples and case studies provided. Some of the examples are fictional to describe the work.

© 2020, Cathy Caswell, The Healthy Living Plan®
1500 Waverley Rd, Waverley, Nova Scotia, Canada

ISBN (paperback): 978-0-9950215-1-8
ISBN (electronic book): 978-0-9950215-2-5

The word *Logosynthesis®* is a registered trademark and used with the permission of its founder, Dr. Willem Lammers. *The Healthy Living Plan®* is a registered trademark owned by the author. The ® is intended when these terms are used throughout this book.

No part of this publication may be reproduced in whole or in part; stored in a retrieval system; or transmitted in any form or by any means, electronic, mechanical, photocopying, recording, or otherwise without written permission of the author. Any requests for reproducing any part of this book should be directed to:

Cathy Caswell, 1500 Waverley Rd, Waverley, Nova Scotia B2R 1W7

Cover and interior design by David W. Edelstein
Illustrations by Adriana Caswell

Thank you to my family, friends, and colleagues who have supported me to explore beyond my comfort zone for new understanding.

Thank you to Adriana Caswell for designing the illustrations to creatively describe key concepts.

A very special thank you to Willem Lammers for the wonderful gift of Logosynthesis.
It is with awe and intrigue that
I share what I have learned.

Enjoy!

Foreword

WE'RE LIVING IN FASCINATING TIMES. For some people, this fascination is tightly connected to fear; for others, it shows that we can make a change, departing from what's not perfect in the world we live in. It's a challenge to keep our minds clear in the flood of information reaching our senses. The current situation is challenging us all at a deep level. No human now alive has ever experienced anything like it.

It's interesting to see how people react to the multiple crises of the moment, and how they attempt to reduce the complexity of a situation in which nothing is clear or secure. Most specialists—physicians, mathematicians, epidemiologists, psychologists, economists— tend to focus on what they know from their own discipline. They understand new events from the theory, the methods, and the history of their professional background. This mechanism is not especially useful when it comes to finding your own stance in the face of the current events.

In these times, you are forced to realize how much of your life energy is bound in structures that seemed to offer safety. You don't know when lockdown or rebellion will end and what the world will look like afterward. You don't know how we will meet the challenge of climate change. Will your job or your business be the same? Will your relationships be the same? Will you be able to make money and shop, dine, and travel again in the way you were used to?

In this overwhelming context, each of us must find ways to think, feel, and act. In the context of the current circumstances, we see several patterns of how the human mind processes this new information:

a. Denial: We tend to deny that something new is happening. We activate thought patterns that have been useful as an explanation and as guidelines in the past. People on one side of the political and religious spectrum might believe that this is God's punishment for the recognition of LGBTQ ways of living; elsewhere on this spectrum, a connection between the appearance of the coronavirus and 5G is envisioned. Everybody sees their existing beliefs confirmed.

b. Coping: In times of severe distress, the mind takes to evolutionary patterns of coping with the perceived source of the distress. The lack of experienced safety is met with archaic survival behavior. If the culture puts a heavy emphasis on cleanliness, people will hoard disinfectants and toilet tissue, and if self-defense has a high priority, people will buy guns.

c. Compliance: A third way to create a predictable world is to find a substitute parent who will tell people how

Foreword

to think and what to do to restore safety in a world that has been shaken up by the unknown. People suddenly start to comply with government directives. In that context, it's disturbing that some elected officials grab their chance to establish a dictatorial regime.

d. Blocking: The mind doesn't process the new information; it gets stuck in reaction patterns designed during evolution when enemies were animals and competing tribes, and danger could be met with "fight, flight and freeze." You could attack the enemy and avert the threat, run away from it, or surrender and be killed, flooding your body with endorphins to guarantee a painless transition to the eternal hunting fields.

None of the above mechanisms serves adult, responsible individuals in times of an epidemic. Stories based on these patterns fill the news and social media. They may help to create some safety, but they don't help you to come to your senses to manage the new in the now. So how can you start to feel, think, and act on a higher level than the patterns dictated by evolution?

Cathy Caswell's second book introduces you to Logosynthesis, a new system for healing and development, based on the power of words. She describes how you can identify and understand issues that bind your energy in memories, fantasies, and beliefs. Not only that: she shows you how to free the energy in the service of your mission in life. Applying Logosynthesis may help you in these difficult times because it is designed to resolve the bound energy in your mind and reconnect you to what cannot be destroyed by even the most adverse circumstances: Essence. Your Essence.

Under stress, your connection to Essence is easily disrupted because the intensity of the experience of broken patterns is simply too high. Environmental stress leads to fear and anger on many levels, and these emotions tend to sabotage the higher brain functions you need to think about the situation and act upon the facts—pleasant or unpleasant, easy or challenging.

This book can help you shift from a position in which you're stuck in what you *should* do or *should have* done—or what others should do or should have done—to reconnect to what you really are and develop means to live your purpose. Clearing your path from frozen memories, irrational fantasies, and limiting beliefs will help you discover what you can do now to move forward and accomplish your mission on planet Earth.

Thriving in our times is the result of a process. You have to let go, to say goodbye to everything that won't be the same again. You have to accept that you've lost resources that were available before, that you can no longer freely travel whenever you want, that people who could help you aren't there anymore. You have to accept that you were not prepared for these times, that the power of the people who represent you in government is limited, and that they may make bad decisions. You have to accept that your ability to

Foreword

change things is limited and that you don't know all the factors required to make a decision with a predictable result. That can be painful.

The other, more uplifting, part of the process is to discover your mission and to access new resources to accomplish it: new friends, new colleagues, new forms of working online, unique circumstances. They may invite you to explore who you are and what you're here for in this world.

Thriving means living in the present in the service of your mission in this life. That's not easy, and no one is going to promise you a rose garden, but you can recognize and explore your potential, and you can overcome the blocks on the path to realizing it.

Bad Ragaz, Switzerland, in the summer of that
unpredictable year 2020,
Dr. Willem Lammers

Contents

Foreword ix

Chapter 1: Our world can change in an instant . . . 1
Understanding our reactions 3
Feeling our discomfort 10
Understanding our pain 13
Moving forward 16
How Logosynthesis can help 19
Why Logosynthesis? 31
About this book 45

Chapter 2: Navigating the change 51
A perspective on change 53
A focus on interaction 56
Individuals and change 59
Groups and change 62
Clearing a path forward 68

Chapter 3: Introducing Logosynthesis 79
How Logosynthesis works 81
Learning to use the Basic Procedure 91
The Empty Chair exercise 99
Learning what professionals are saying 101

Chapter 4: Logosynthesis in action 107
Sharing our stories 109
Case Study 1: Overcoming fear 112

Case Study 2: Creating willingness 118
Case Study 3: Resolving tension 124
Case Study 4: Setting boundaries 127
Case Study 5: Focusing attention 132
Case Study 6: Resolving a panic attack 138
Case Study 7: Breathing through grief 143
Case Study 8: Calming distress related to trauma 146
Case Study 9: Eliminating a teacher's frustration 150
Case Study 10: Building a student's confidence 154
Case Study 11: Self-coaching during times of transition 158
Case Study 12: Letting go of the need to fight so hard 162

Chapter 5: Integrating Logosynthesis into everyday living 167

Thriving in my everyday life 169
Supporting you to thrive in everyday life 175
Clearing your path for action 198
An illustrated guide 211
Having impact in our groups 220

Conclusion 229

Appendix 237

Glossary of terms in Logosynthesis® 239
Books on Logosynthesis® 245
Additional Resources on Logosynthesis® 246

About the Author 249

THRIVING IN OUR TIMES

CHAPTER 1

Our world can change in an instant

*We feel the intensity of it all,
even when it is hard to name what we are experiencing.
The discomfort that gets triggered by
our situation is a key reason that
we benefit from learning how to resolve what bothers us
to thrive in our times.*

Understanding our reactions

We want to enjoy our lives but we are often not aware of how our patterns of reacting get in the way of taking meaningful action. Our reactions are how we act and feel in response to something that happens. We have an opportunity to learn to use this information to resolve what causes our distress and keeps us stuck in habitual patterns of behavior. This is especially helpful during times of change and uncertainty. As we learn to resolve what bothers us, we can more fully enjoy healthy living and we can embrace extraordinary living. The following definitions highlight two key terms I use throughout this book:

Healthy:
enjoying good health;
showing physical, mental, and emotional well-being

Extraordinary:
going beyond what is usual, regular, or customary;
employed for or sent on a special service or mission

— Merriam-Webster Dictionary —

We enjoy healthy living when we feel well: physically, mentally, and emotionally. We enjoy extraordinary living when we are able to move beyond our normal routines to feel connected to our unique mission in life. In this book, I will share how I learned to use Logosynthesis, developed by Dr. Willem Lammers, to feel an increased sense of clarity to take meaningful action in my everyday life, during times of change and uncertainty. I was able to recognize that as I felt calmer in my responses, those around me benefited.

Your experiences and responses are different from mine. I will show you how to use this one method so that you can learn to resolve what bothers you to feel better. You will learn to appreciate the power of changing your reactions to help you to thrive in our times and to create a supportive environment for others.

We all experience times when our comfortable routines are disrupted and our beliefs are challenged. We are called to move beyond our routine patterns of thinking and acting. We are faced with conditions that are new and unfamiliar and we have no opportunity to gradually adjust. How we respond to these unusual circumstances impacts our wellbeing and the wellbeing of those around us. We can easily get stuck in distressing patterns of thought and emotions that are anchored in our beliefs and past experiences.

In this book, I provide a perspective on how we, as humans, respond when our lives suddenly change. I describe how these automatic responses can further add to our distress. I then introduce Logosynthesis and show how to use this model to change patterns of reactions. I also present a series of cases studies, written by an international group of coaches, counselors, and therapists trained in Logosynthesis. The case studies demonstrate how this one fast and easy method can be used for healing and personal development. I outline five pillars to support healthy living and offer a guide to help embrace extraordinary living. You will begin to experience more ease in your life by resolving what bothers you before you take action. A glossary of terms and further information about Logosynthesis is available in the Appendix.

To start, let's consider where we have been. In early 2020, we experienced the start of a global pandemic. Similar pandemics have happened before. We were warned that it could happen again and we had an idea of the crisis that would occur. Yet even as the stories about the virus began to surface, we occupied ourselves with the demands and desires of our everyday lives. We had no comprehension of the speed and intensity of change that was ahead of us. We were busy living our ordinary lives in our ordinary ways.

In a very short period of time, our lives shifted dramatically. As the virus spread around the globe, our normal routines were disrupted amid fear and uncertainty. We were told to stay at home and avoid social interactions. Businesses shut their doors. Stock markets plummeted. Healthcare and other essential workers no longer felt safe in their jobs. Our minds could not process how everything could happen so fast.

We became obsessed with the media as we watched the number of Covid-19 cases rise. Millions of people contracted the virus. Millions of people lost their jobs. Governments scrambled to provide billions and trillions of dollars in aid. As the weeks turned into months, we noticed more unrest. People were having difficulty reopening their businesses. People grew tired of staying at home. People didn't feel safe going back out in public. We were witness to more distressing events, including racial injustices and police brutality. Protests and riots called for action to end long-standing inequity.

This period is one example of intense change and uncertainty on a global scale. Other extraordinary events include global recessions, climate change, and technological advances. We also experience exceptional events on a smaller scale. Our workplaces may downsize. Our community may experience catastrophic weather, such as a hurricane. We also experience times of intense change and uncertainty on an individual basis. This can include an accident, the death of a loved one, getting married, and having children. During these times, we move beyond our comfort zone. Our normal routines and habitual patterns are challenged.

When times are normal, we tend to go about our daily routines without thinking. We do what is expected of us by our families, our friends, and society at large. We are often unaware that we are operating based on patterns of frozen reactions, which are triggered by frozen perceptions. Triggers, frozen reactions and frozen perceptions are defined in Logosynthesis terms and available in the Glossary (see Appendix). The terms are also illustrated as follows:

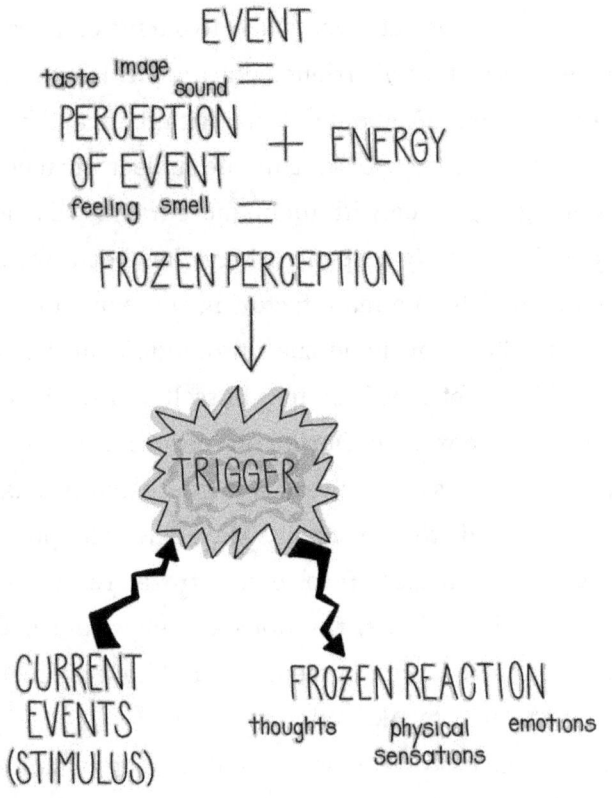

When we operate according to our programmed responses, it can be difficult to get in touch with what inspires us, what moves us to create change. We may sense some unresolved tension yet we may be unaware of what is missing in our lives. We may also desire to move beyond our routines and our cultural norms but we sense something uncomfortable that holds us in place.

For example, Jack loves food, cooking, and travel but his long-time friends like to stay close to home and are focused on building things. Jack would love to pursue culinary training. He senses that his friends don't get it. He doesn't feel comfortable talking about cooking with them and his voice wavers when he tries to bring up the subject. He feels stuck between going along with them and pursuing his passion. He decides to study carpentry. Maya has been working in her current role in a manufacturing company for the past five years. She wants to pursue a promotion but she is nervous and her subtle self-talk tells herself that she is not prepared for the next step. During her performance appraisal, she tells her boss that she is not interested in changing positions at this time. Jack and Maya have an opportunity to use Logosynthesis to resolve their frozen reactions. They can use their thoughts, emotions and physical sensations to resolve their frozen perceptions and have an increased feeling of clarity to take action.

There is a strong invisible pull to keep us connected with who and what we know. I experienced this when I started to learn about Logosynthesis. I operated within a cultural norm of hard work, resilience, and helping others: "Be strong and carry on!" I was comfortable in my network of family and friends who shared these values. When I began to explore Logosynthesis, I was introduced to a new group of people with different ideas about how I could help others. I had to move beyond my comfort zone to learn new information. For example, I was introduced to the importance of healing rather than simply carrying on. At first, I had difficulty in explaining what I had learned to family, friends, and coworkers. My new understanding was shifting my beliefs beyond my group norms. It did not always feel comfortable. And these were still "ordinary" times!

Our frozen reactions are even less helpful when our world is rapidly changing. Our experiences may not always be comfortable. We react and this triggers others to react. If we have elderly parents who were alone during the pandemic and we saw images in the media of elderly people in nursing homes, this could trigger a frozen reaction that is associated with intense guilt and a strong desire to change the situation. Depending on the nature of our situation, we may experience a wide range of responses, such as grief, disappointment, or frustration. While we have a variety of coping methods, the intensity of our response may result in an overload. Our lives may feel out of control.

This book will show how you can learn to use Logosynthesis to notice your distressing thoughts, emotions, and body symptoms. These are the frozen reactions that bother you. Rather than learning to cope with or avoid these reactions, you will learn to let go of these automatic responses. You may think it is your boss, your spouse or strangers that bother you. It is a frozen perception that gets triggered, which results in distressing thoughts, emotions, and body sensations. When we learn to resolve the triggers, others no longer have the power to bother us. They simply are present and we no longer react to them. We are free to act.

Logosynthesis is a model that supports healing and development, offering one method that can be used to both help you heal from distressing memories and feel confident to embrace new challenges. As you use Logosynthesis routinely, you will notice a shift toward feelings of calm, clarity, and focus. You will feel more energized with a sense of purpose. To begin, let's take a look at how this discomfort and pain may appear in your life.

Feeling our discomfort

Different people had different responses to the early stages of the global pandemic. When we were told to stay home, some of us appreciated a quieter lifestyle. Others could not tolerate quiet. Some of us had more time to enjoy family dinners. Others did not have food to put on the table. Some of us enjoyed the comfort of being with family. Others did not feel safe at home. Some of us worked extremely hard in unsafe spaces. Others stayed home with little to do.

We looked to our leaders to give assurance that we

would manage together. Yet we experienced feelings of worry, fear, grief, and anxiety. Often, it was hard to get in touch with what we were feeling. We may have experienced a general heaviness or exhaustion. We may have noticed a weird and unsettled vibe. We may have been unable to concentrate.

When we were asked to stay at home, we may have distracted ourselves with Facebook, Netflix, and e-sports. We may have turned to medications, alcohol, or drugs to calm our edge. We may have found our Zen through yoga, meditation, or running. For many, conversations with family and friends helped to feel connected. At times we may have simply lost our cool. And yes, it may have felt good to let it out!

When we were allowed to go out again, many of us felt eager to get back to work and to get together with our friends. Yet we realized that we enjoyed the comfort of home. For some, heading back to the shops and to work didn't feel safe. The uncertainty and added rules created discomfort. It was easy to feel anxious because people around us weren't obeying the rules. Our world wasn't like before the pandemic and we sensed discomfort.

While our individual situations may have felt intense, we then added a constant stream of stories shared through the media. We knew that many people were suffering in our community, in our country, and around the globe. We could feel the unease, even when it was hard to name what we were experiencing.

Then another level of discomfort began to surface. We needed people to own their actions and their reactions. Each of us needed to be responsible for our own behavior because of the huge impact it had on the lives of others. It was easy to feel triggered when we worked hard to follow the rules and saw others openly disregard them. Everyone needed to do their part yet we were not in control of how others acted. We were not able to have funerals yet we saw long lines of people at Costco. We kept our children away from their friends yet others met in groups at the beach. We worked hard to follow the rules and it bothered us when others did not.

In Canada, we have grown up in a time when we have been generally able to do what we wanted, when we wanted. During the pandemic, suddenly our actions could have a life or death impact on others. Our governments told us we could not go to the beach. We could not have birthday parties. We could not get a haircut. We were triggered.

We started to notice a series of actions and reactions. The reactions were emotionally charged with fear, worry, and panic. We experienced physical reactions such as tightness in our chest, pounding headaches, and exhaustion. Words were uttered that felt harsh. People acted in ways that did not feel kind and compassionate. These responses triggered further distressing reactions in others. We knew the rule that every action has an equal and opposite reaction. Yet at times, the reactions felt much more intense than the initial action. We could feel discomfort and, in some cases, we even felt pain.

Understanding our pain

There is no questioning the seriousness of the global pandemic. While some of us were able to recharge during this time, many felt discomfort related to change and uncertainty. Others experienced intense pain and suffering.

If we had experienced distressing situations in the past, the conditions of the pandemic may have automatically triggered frozen perceptions of past events, resulting in frozen reactions with the same intensity of the initial event. In other words, the thoughts, emotions, and body sensations we experienced during the pandemic may not have been directly related to the events of the pandemic. When distressing memories are activated, we experience an immediate, energetic response. It bypasses our rational thinking. We may describe an inability to breathe, an extreme pressure in the chest, or a shooting pain. At times, the pain can feel unbearable and we don't know how to stop it. We struggle because others do not experience it. We can be in the same place yet having very different experiences.

Discomfort and pain provide us with information. Our automatic responses are energetic and part of our survival instincts. In Logosynthesis terms, a current event activates a frozen perception, which triggers a frozen reaction.

We recognize the perceptions as memories, beliefs, and fantasies and they keep us connected to our culture and norms during ordinary times. They can also activate fight-flight-freeze mode. When our world suddenly changes, our frozen perceptions trigger powerful, distressing responses to encourage us to return to normal. When we are unable to change our world, it can be beneficial to learn how to change how we react to our world.

You may be more familiar of thinking of the sequence of stimulus and response. As you read the sequence below, notice the intensity of your individual response and be aware of how others may respond based on their previous experiences.

Think of the phrase, "a busy emergency room filled with patients on ventilators." What are your thoughts? What are your emotions? How does your body respond? You can compare your response to what you think Caroline and Matt would experience based on the following description.

Caroline worked in an emergency room in New York during the height of the pandemic. She and her husband are both doctors. They decided to leave their children with her sister in Baltimore because they didn't want to risk getting them sick. Caroline worked long hours in the crowded ER. She frequently had to put patients on ventilators. Several patients died each day. The sights, sounds, and smells were intense.

Matt was busy working from home in a sales job during

this period. He sold personal care products to major retailers. Suddenly, his days were busy trying to fill orders for hand sanitizers and disinfectants. Although he spent hours on the phone, he was able to enjoy listening to his favorite music and eating his favorite foods.

We can expect that Caroline will have a much stronger reaction than Matt to the thought of an emergency room. If both Caroline and Matt were to walk into an emergency room today, we can also expect that Caroline will reactivate her experience during the pandemic. We can expect that Matt may simply respond to what is happening around him in the moment.

Previous life experiences will influence how we experience our current situations, especially when our world is rapidly changing. The current situation will reactivate painful sensations from a previous distressing situation. Consider the following examples:

- If your parent lost their job when you were a young child, you may have a vivid memory of that experience. You experience an intense fear of losing your job during the pandemic.
- If you had strict lessons that you should "always play by the rules," you may hear that voice in your head. You may react strongly when you see people disrespecting the rules during the pandemic.
- If you experienced a significant failure because you were not organized and prepared, you may be triggered and feel

frustrated working from home if you are surrounded by a busy family during the pandemic.

As we look to thrive in our times, it is important to appreciate that we each respond differently. While I experience enjoyment, you may feel discomfort or pain in the exact same setting, or vice versa. We each move forward influenced by our past experiences.

Moving forward

As we move through periods of change and uncertainty, we want to get back to normal. Yet our experience of everyday life may feel very different. We can't go back to what we had. For some, the changes may be subtle. For others, the difference feels heavy. We go forward with memories that now influence how we feel in our everyday life. At times we are not even aware of how our past experience impacts us. Some examples of what we might experience are:

- I shouldn't feel so exhausted but I do.
- I can't focus or concentrate on my work.
- People around me are driving me crazy!
- I am terrified that I am going to lose everything that I own.
- I can't breathe when I think about what lies ahead.
- I panic trying to figure out how I am going to get this company back on track.

- I am extremely worried about how my children are coping.
- I am going to live for today because I could have died!

We desire that, as time passes, we will feel better. Time alone does not heal the past, especially under distressing circumstances. The frozen perceptions that trigger our distress are energetic. Our rational mind cannot process the pain and suffering. We learn to cope, to change our situation or to simply do nothing. We move forward, each with our own memories that we carry with us.

For example, Tracey experienced challenges adjusting to working from home after having worked for a long time in an office setting. She didn't have a dedicated space and she had young children at home. She had trouble walking away from the computer at the end of the day. She felt frustrated when she had to help her children with school work during the day. She felt guilty that work was disrupted so she worked harder and longer hours. She was worried about her children. She was also easily frustrated when they needed attention. And she felt out of sorts because she was missing the connection with coworkers who could relate to her situation. She was adapting to new routines but she could feel sharp pains in her temples. She was easily frustrated and she kept thinking: "I want my old life back!" Tracey's partner and her children also wanted her to have her old life back.

Tracey's reactions to the situation provided information that could be used to help her feel better. When we learn to recognize our frozen reactions by noticing our thoughts, emotions, and body sensations, we can learn to identify the frozen perceptions that trigger these responses. These painful memories, limiting beliefs and fantasies for the future are the triggers that can be changed using the power of three specific sentences used in Logosynthesis. The following illustration outlines the work:

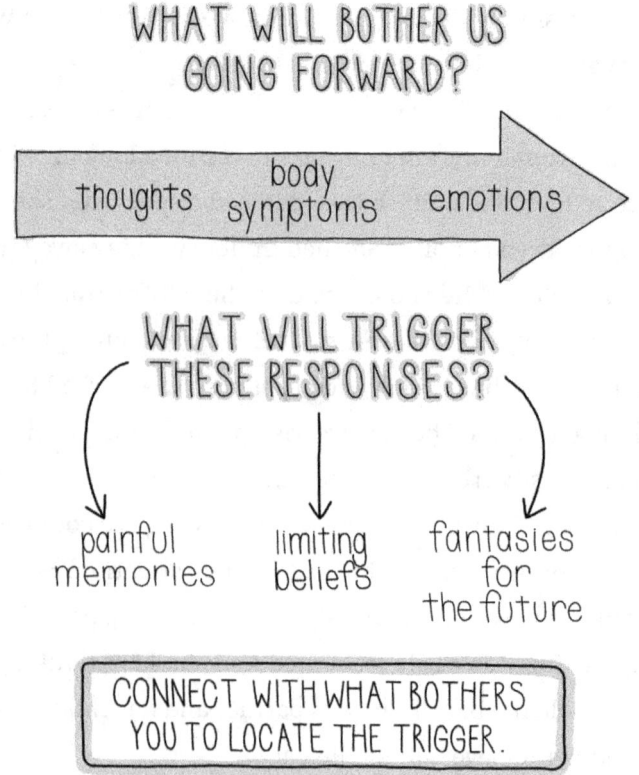

How Logosynthesis can help

Our definitions of health encompass body, mind, and spirit. Humans have a long history of trying to understand how mind and body are connected to spirit. We have created many narratives to help us with our understanding and these narratives have formed our beliefs and rituals. During childhood, we learn many life lessons through experience and teaching. These lessons are stored as frozen perceptions which continue to influence us into adulthood. These frozen perceptions are responsible for our patterns of reacting but they do not always trigger distress. When the narratives and the beliefs are not able to evolve with our times and as we learn and grow, this frozen energy leads to blocks and suffering.

Our families, institutions, and societies are held together in an energy field. This energetic structure holds our collective experiences and beliefs. This is our culture. As new experiences occur, new perceptions are formed which shift the culture over time yet the old patterns continue to influence individuals in groups. This energy shapes the norms of our families, our workplaces, our communities, and our societies. We adopt the beliefs and norms of society, often without being aware of the programming.

Life can feel great when we are comfortable in our surroundings. We might enjoy a good job, a beautiful family, and a lovely home. We adopt the norms of our community.

In Western society, we are conditioned to recognize that if we get an education and work hard, we will be rewarded. We are able to buy more of what makes us feel good. We share with others who are less fortunate. Life is good.

When we do not fit the perceived norms, life may not feel so good. We may not be able to get a job. We may feel different from those around us. We may not feel that we are achieving what is expected. Distressing thoughts, emotions, and body sensations will provide feedback that our experience does not match the patterns of society. We can use Logosynthesis to identify and shift our reactions to relieve feelings of distress. The norms of society will no longer trigger us to feel bad. We can embrace that we are different and we are better able to simply enjoy what is meaningful in our lives.

We may also find ourselves in a position where we are well respected in society but our world changes instantly. A pandemic can suddenly hit. Our routine patterns are disrupted and we feel discomfort or pain. We may be a celebrated chef yet we feel lost when no one can dine out. We may be a respected emergency room doctor who performs well under pressure yet we are overwhelmed by the number of people dying under our care. We may be recognized as a caring politician yet we struggle to make difficult decisions because we are not able to help everyone in need. While life may feel good when conditions are normal, an abrupt change in our circumstances can leave us feeling distressed.

Our world can change in an instant

Willem Lammers developed Logosynthesis as a guided-change model to support healing and development. It offers a simple and powerful method to shift how we react to what bothers us. By recognizing the power of words to shift energy, we can restore the flow of energy to connect with what is meaningful in our lives.

The foundation for Logosynthesis is the understanding that we are Essence. We are life energy born with a life purpose. Essence is energy in flow and does not suffer. Life experiences result in frozen perceptions that we recognize as painful memories, limiting beliefs, and fantasies of how our life should be. These frozen perceptions trigger frozen reactions which result in distressing, reactive patterns. We experience suffering.

*Our true Self does not suffer.
We suffer because the awareness of our Essence is lost.*

This excerpt from *Self Coaching with Logosynthesis®* (Lammers, 2015) offers a wonderful starting point to begin to feel better. Using Logosynthesis, we can learn how to restore the flow of our Essence, our life energy. During times of change and uncertainty, our reactions provide signals that something may be stuck. We can use this information to identify the energetic block and use the three Logosynthesis sentences to move beyond our frozen reactions.

In Logosynthesis, three sentences have been specifically formulated, based on an understanding of psychology, psychotherapy, energy, and spirituality, to restore our connection to Essence. Working at this level, we can experience surprising relief from our distress and suffering. I continue to be amazed that when we begin with the recognition of Essence, all types of distress may be relieved with unexplainable speed and simplicity. This is perhaps best understood from a spiritual context.

If we are living in our world without an awareness of Essence, we may sense that our lives are missing something. We may feel lethargic or bored. We may lack the energy to pursue what is important. We lose connection with what gives meaning to our lives. If we operate solely from Essence, we may feel good but we have little impact on our world. It is when we connect with Essence in our everyday lives that we can embrace our uniqueness and thrive. As we recognize what bothers us and restore the flow of our creative energy, more of our life energy is accessible to us.

In *Logosynthesis: Enjoying Life More Fully* (Caswell, 2017), I made specific note that my story was about finding peace and contentment right where I was. I had read a lot of books about people escaping their lives to create something new. Those stories demonstrated that we have the power to take action to achieve something better and to create the life we desire. While many of those stories were certainly inspiring, I was not interested in removing myself from my life.

I simply wanted to let go of the intensity of some of my reactive patterns so that I could focus on what was important to me and to enjoy life more fully. And that is exactly what I have experienced.

Logosynthesis provides me with clarity to take meaningful action. More of my energy is available for the things that are important to me. I am better able to respond in my everyday life, even when times are challenging.

Logosynthesis works by recognizing that throughout our life, we create frozen perceptions known as memories, beliefs, and fantasies about how life should be. When the frozen perception is activated by events in the present, it triggers the same automatic response as the initial event. The trigger produces frozen reactions, which shape what we know to be true. Our frozen reactions are our survival instincts. They also provide us with information that something is wrong. We recognize this as distressing thoughts, emotions and body sensations. For example, if a car ran a red light and hit us, we may experience the same tension or sharp pain every time we go through an intersection. We may also have the image or the sound of the crash replaying in our mind, triggering other distressing feelings.

We also experience triggers as beliefs or limiting beliefs. My belief that I need to work hard has been shaped by experiences in my childhood. I witnessed my parents working hard, through many adverse conditions. I feel that I don't need to question whether I should work or not because I know that hard work is important. And I know that when I am not working hard, I can feel guilty or lazy. I have also managed to pass along this attitude to my children.

This belief is beneficial to help me earn a living so that I can enjoy a comfortable lifestyle. I know what has to be done and I do it. However, in certain situations, this belief can activate intense responses which negatively impact me and those around me.

I worked for Kraft Foods for many years, when suddenly the company was purchased by Heinz. The new management introduced significant changes and we were all asked to work harder. I felt triggered because I was already working really hard. I was frustrated and annoyed because senior management should have known that the expectations were not reasonable. I was quick to defend our team and my tone did not always feel kind and compassionate. Over time, I learned to use Logosynthesis to tone down my responses. In most cases, the triggers related to my experience while growing up on a busy farm. I used the three sentences specific to Logosynthesis to shift the energy (I explain these sentences in detail in Chapter 3). This allowed me to calm my reactions and to focus on the task at hand.

Learning how Logosynthesis could help me during this sudden change in my life proved to be extremely helpful during the global pandemic. We were all asked to stay home. In our household, there wasn't a lot of work that I had to do. I know that my normal response would be to work hard anyway. If there wasn't work to do, I would create something to keep busy. Because I had already resolved many of these triggers relating to working hard, I didn't feel as compelled to clean the house, cook all the meals, and find things for my daughters to do. I was able to focus on my writing and training and to allow my family to focus on what was important to them, while still considering family responsibilities. I continue to value hard work but it feels calmer. I am better able to focus on work that is meaningful to me.

Logosynthesis can help to find relief for anything that bothers us. The thought of a needle or of delivering a presentation can trigger intense feelings for some people. Others have no reaction or only a slight response. We often recognize these reactions as irrational, meaning these triggers override our rational thinking. We are unable to think our way to relief. We learn to cope with the response. Using Logosynthesis, the issue dissipates and it no longer bothers us in the future. The guided method eliminates the trigger so we no longer experience the distressing response. We no longer require coping strategies nor do we need to avoid situations. We can donate blood without being triggered by a fear of needles. We can deliver an important presentation without worrying about what could happen.

As we work with Logosynthesis, we learn to appreciate that it is a very gentle and compassionate process. It really is about simply letting go of attachments. As humans, we connect through powerful emotional bonds. If we think of letting go of these bonds that structure our normal lives, we can activate painful memories, limiting beliefs, and fantasies about what could happen. We often don't want to let go of our pain and grief because it feels that we are leaving behind something that is very important to us. We don't want to let go of our conviction that others need to do things differently, for example, because we believe that we are doing everything correctly. We feel that we can't let go of a stressful job or toxic friendship because we are attached.

The thought of letting go can be very uncomfortable when we are conditioned to hold on to the things that are familiar in our lives. The thought can also be uncomfortable for very practical reasons, such as the need for a job to pay bills. It can be difficult to let go when we don't know what comes next. When we let go of the distressing thoughts, we are free to let things happen. We may discover that the job no longer feels stressful, we feel confident to embrace a different challenge or we feel that we can embrace the challenge of the current situation.

This reference to "Let it go" simply means releasing the energy that is stuck: the triggers. When our energy is frozen, there is resistance. There is no flow. We are trapped in a mode of reacting rather than creating. When we let go of the pain of grief, we reconnect with our Essence. When we let go of the rigidity of our beliefs, we can appreciate what others have to offer. When we let go of the tension from holding on too tight, we can trust to take the next step forward.

In the past five years, I have applied Logosynthesis to support many important decisions. In two instances, I made the decision to let go of roles that felt important to me. In each case, it was not a quick or easy decision. My initial response was that I should continue in my role but I also recognized that the roles were limiting other areas of my life that were important. I didn't know what would happen but I was able to let go of my attachment to the outcome. I trusted that the decision would create an opportunity for new learning and growth.

I have come to appreciate that letting go is not about leaving things behind. It is about opening up to new possibilities rather than holding on too tightly. It is about trusting to let our children go out to explore the world. It is about feeling comfortable to let others do their jobs and helping them feel supported along the way. It is about feeling confident that even though we may experience very significant challenges in life, we will learn and grow from the experience.

Magic happens when we can remain open, especially during times of change and uncertainty. Our challenge will be to maintain trust when we feel uncertain. We require boundaries to offer support but the boundaries may shift. Our space may not feel safe, both physically and emotionally. We can use Logosynthesis to help us trust, feel confident, and create space to explore. We can learn to let go of what gets in the way of taking action. We can free our creative energy so it becomes available for things which bring us meaning and joy.

Through self-coaching or with a trained guide, we can use Logosynthesis routinely to feel better. When the trigger is resolved, the distress is gone and it does not come back. It doesn't change what happened but it does shift how we feel about what happened. We are better able to realize our own power and move forward.

The following incident provides an example of how I used Logosynthesis during the pandemic to feel better. My daughter Adriana was studying in Germany when the pandemic was declared. We felt comfortable that she was well looked after and our intention was to allow her to stay at school. However, on Friday, March 13th, the Prime Minister of Canada declared that all Canadians travelling abroad should return home as soon as possible although anyone with symptoms of Covid-19 would not be permitted onto their flights. Further, if Adriana left the school for quarantine reasons, she would not be allowed back on campus. We felt comfortable with her at school but the direction was to return to Canada while flights were still available. The space between school and home certainly did not feel safe. I thought: "What if she has symptoms at the airport and they don't let her on the plane?" I felt worried and edgy as she started her journey home. I used

Logosynthesis to feel better. I connected with the thoughts, emotions, and body sensations. I used a rating scale called SUDS to rate my distress on a scale from 0 to 10, with 0 being no distress and 10 being the most distressing (I explain this more fully in Chapter 3). I rated it a 6. I stayed with this distress. I had a perception of Adriana in the airport. I labeled this as the trigger to use in the sentences. I said the three Logosynthesis sentences below, with a pause after each sentence to allow the words to work. This is known as a cycle of Logosynthesis, as follows:

- *I retrieve all my energy bound up in this "image of Adriana in the airport" and take it to the right place in my Self.*
- *Working pause.*
- *I remove all non-me energy related to this "image of Adriana in the airport" from all of my cells, all of my body and my personal space, and send it to where it truly belongs.*
- *Working pause.*
- *I retrieve all of my energy bound up in all of my reactions to this "image of Adriana in the airport" and take it to the right place in my Self.*
- *Working pause.*

My level of distress dropped to a 1. I felt calmer and the edginess was gone. I trusted that she was healthy and that she would find her way on to the plane. There was nothing I had to do. I sent her a text to have a good trip and went to sleep.

I know it was normal to feel anxious given the situation. I also know that, normally, I would recognize that the situation would pass and we would move on. However, I was aware that when I feel anxious, I am more likely to check-in repeatedly with my daughter. She would feel this vibe and it would impact her ability to enjoy her trip home, at a time when she was already disappointed and upset about having to leave her school unexpectedly. I recognized that how I responded would impact her experience. I know that when I am able to feel calm, she is better able to feel calm.

As the pandemic gained momentum, I was not personally worried about catching the virus but I noticed that I was concerned about the negative impact the pandemic would have on a global level. I could feel an uncomfortable vibe because I was aware of the dangers around health, economics, and social unrest. I thought that I should be doing something but I didn't know what to do, especially given the direction to stay at home. I used Logosynthesis to help me to focus on writing. I felt calmer in my conversations with my family as we made decisions around physical distancing. I recognized that I was not in a position to change the new rules or to control the actions of others but I was able to change how I responded in situations.

With physical distancing, I had an increased opportunity for online training and collaboration with my colleagues. I noticed a very common theme through our shared learning. We were using Logosynthesis to feel calmer and more focused during this period of change and uncertainty. We were using it as a very targeted approach to help us feel better and to gain clarity about what was important in our lives. I was reminded why Logosynthesis initially appealed to me during a very busy time in my life.

Why Logosynthesis?

In 2013, I met a cousin, Dr. Willem Lammers. He was visiting Canada from Switzerland to offer training in Logosynthesis. Another cousin had suggested that we meet. I am always curious to learn what family members are doing and his work intrigued me. I was already intrigued by the works of Hay House and other spiritual authors, such as Louise Hay, Dr. Wayne Dyer, Abraham and Ester Hicks, Gregg Braden, and more. In many ways, Willem's work was aligned to these teachings and I was curious to learn.

Willem's approach is based in psychology, psychotherapy, spirituality, and energy-healing methods. He presents a simple, self-coachable yet powerful model which can be easily repeated to relieve many types of distress and support healing and development. I appreciated that the fast and easy technique Willem taught was anchored with a profound and compassionate theory.

When I told my friends about Logosynthesis, many viewed it as simply another coping or stress-management technique. I knew that the model offered more than a technique. This was new understanding about how we, as humans, can access our higher power to heal and to thrive in our everyday lives, especially during times of change and uncertainty.

I have often wondered why I was immediately intrigued by Logosynthesis and why I have sustained that interest. I realized that, in many ways, Willem reminds me of my two Dutch uncles who were priests. One uncle supported missionary work in Tanzania for fifty years. The other uncle was a parish priest and an author in Belgium. I always enjoyed their visits to Canada and they held a special place in my family. They encouraged me to challenge my beliefs. When I became stuck in my point of view, I would notice a smile to remind me that I held an interesting belief. They also highlighted that religion changes with the times to meet the needs of the people and yet we stay connected to our spirituality. When I met Willem, his accent, his appearance, and his intellect reminded me of them. I was inspired to challenge my beliefs by connecting with my spirituality.

In 2013, I was experiencing a very busy time in my personal life. I was working full-time, my children were active in sports and 4-H, I volunteered in several organizations, my husband and I owned a pharmacy, and the list goes on. Life was very busy and it kept getting busier. Things were great but I often felt triggered and reacted in ways I didn't like. To be clear, I did not feel that I was doing anything wrong. My agitation was often related to *others* doing things differently from how I thought things should be done. In some cases, others simply didn't do what I expected they should do. I felt the problem was with other people and that I had to fix things or help them do things the right way. I wanted to feel calmer without losing focus on what was important. I wanted to ease some of the pressure that I felt to do it all.

Now, having used Logosynthesis on a regular basis for more than five years, I do feel a greater sense of calm and clarity. Many of the distractions, complaints, and irritants have simply fallen away. I am better able to trust my decisions. I don't feel that I need to rush through my work. I don't feel the same need to control situations. I more fully enjoy my relationships, especially with my family. Certainly, I still get triggered but I know that it doesn't have to become a pattern of reactive behavior. I am more empowered to choose my response. I am less stuck in my reactions. The more I realized that I had the power to change my reactions, I could stop trying to change others and change situations. My life now feels easier and simply flows better.

My interest in sharing Willem's work is to inspire you to experience how this feels. There is a peaceful engagement in life. I am better able to work with others towards a common goal. I am aware of the beauty of simply noticing my responses to what bothers me and resolving my reactions. When I feel better, those around me feel better too. I am aware of the power of my influence as an individual in my family, my workplace, and my community.

My education and work experience have helped me to appreciate why Logosynthesis is so unique. My undergraduate degree was a Bachelor of Science in Nutrition and Consumer Studies. This program provided a context to understand healthy living. I learned the science of good nutrition to support health and wellness and learned to recognize healthy eating as one of the components of a healthy lifestyle. I learned about the impact of socio-economic factors on overall health and wellness. I also began to appreciate the power of spirit, energy, and purpose to influence health.

A course in Organizational Behavior held a special interest for me. This was a mandatory business course because our dean recognized the importance of interpersonal relationships in the workplace. I easily recognized the concepts from my experience growing up in a large family on a busy dairy farm. As I entered the work force, I quickly realized that group dynamics have a significant influence on both health and productivity. Through an Executive Masters in Business Administration, I deepened my appreciation for the role of organizational behavior on employee wellbeing and business success. This learning supported me both in my corporate career and in my community involvement.

When I was introduced to Willem, my life was good! I felt engaged at work, my husband and children were doing well and I actively participated in my community. I loved connecting with family and friends. I did not feel that I had issues. I was fine. I was simply having a hard time keeping up with everything that was important to me.

Yet Willem sparked my curiosity. I was aware that we all get triggered in everyday life. I was aware that my behavior can trigger others to react. I knew what it was like when a phone call or an email from head office disrupted the work of the entire office. I knew how parents on the sidelines at a school or club sporting event sucked the fun out of the game for everyone. I knew how coworkers responded to comments that were not intended in the way they were received. I knew how people reacted to the prospect of layoffs. I knew that we certainly didn't all respond in the same way. I knew there was an opportunity to do better but I felt stuck in repetitive thoughts: "I should do more"; "They should listen"; "It's not my responsibility."

Suddenly, I was provided a comprehensive model that had potential to help me let go of these reactive patterns. In *Logosynthesis: Enjoying Life More Fully* (Caswell, 2017), I demonstrate how I began to use Logosynthesis to support my everyday life. I provide examples of applying the technique to resolve everyday situations such as losing my cool as a parent, stress at work, frustration in a relationship, and supporting a friend with a pounding headache. I highlight the barriers I experienced when I started to work with the method and I explain how situations started to shift.

I wrote that book three years ago. Since that time, I have gained certification as a Practitioner and an Instructor in Logosynthesis®. I have a deeper understanding of what is possible from experiences in my own life, in training seminars and in coaching others. I have learned a great deal through my connection with Willem and an international group of professional coaches, counselors, and therapists. Over the course of five years, I have witnessed a beautiful transformation in people who regularly use this model for healing and personal development. I am now much more confident about the impact and significance of what is possible with Logosynthesis. Willem has published more books to aid our understanding of Logosynthesis, as outlined in the Appendix to this book. His latest book, *Discover Logosynthesis®: The Power of Words in Healing and Development* (2020), offers a great introduction to his work.

My commitment to sharing this comprehensive model is also influenced by my past experiences. We all have situations in our lives that challenge us to consider what could have been different if we had access to a different understanding at the time. We experience situations that leave an impact long after the event passes. For me, workplace relationships are very important. I believe that we all show up striving to do the best we can in a challenging environment. We believe that the actions we take are what is needed to do a good job. I recognize that the relationship between a boss and their staff is important. This relationship can create significant levels of distress and dysfunction. At times, difficult decisions are required. These decisions can inspire us to look for better alternatives. I believe that Logosynthesis offers a model to resolve challenging group dynamics in the workplace and could have provided a workable solution in the following example.

I will take you back to my university experience. As I mentioned above, I was introduced to Organizational Behavior by a very dynamic professor and I loved the course. I felt great about the case study I wrote for the final exam. That is, until I was with a group of friends at the university pub and my professor approached me: "Cathy, I don't know how to mark your exam! I don't know if I should give you an A for genius or an F."

I told him that I thought the A would work just fine.

He went on to explain that I had changed the case so he didn't know how to mark it. I was confused and asked for clarification.

"You can't fire the boss!"

I was even more confused at this point. In the case, the boss was clearly the problem.

"Yes, but you can't fire the boss!"

I asked if I had laid out the case well and if my solution was workable.

"Yes, it was genius. But you can't fire the boss."

Although I did not agree, this was my introduction to a very strong "corporate" energy field in which there is no option to fire the boss. Move forward twenty years. I was working in a fast-paced environment with aggressive demands to achieve sales targets and manage promotional budgets. The pressure felt intense. John, my boss, was easily triggered by the demands of his boss and he displayed very reactive behavior. He created a very nervous vibe in the office, making it difficult to feel calm and focus on our work. Over the years, people quit because of the situation. Tensions within relationships were not a secret. We were working in a regional sales office so the situation was less visible at senior levels in head office. However, there was certainly an awareness of behavior patterns because many in senior management had worked directly with John in the past.

The situation was not new, so there was a sense of acceptance: it could not be changed. The grocery industry was changing, the sales department restructured and the sales targets became more challenging. John's nervous behavior intensified. A single, reactive comment easily derailed the entire team. Some people were not in a position to quit but they were highly stressed.

Our team looked for ways to improve the situation but the problem behaviors seemed unchangeable. We were challenged to consider the best way to move forward. The situation was eventually raised with Human Resources and our Vice President. An assessment process was launched to determine if we could work together better and change the disruptive behaviors. We completed several standard workplace assessments to help improve relationships. We were eager to do what was necessary, yet the same reactive behavior patterns persisted. John became more agitated as the business challenges increased. He would hover by our desks and repeatedly ask questions to which there were no answers. The additional fear of losing his job added to the nervous vibe. We were triggered and we were challenged in our responses.

John's reactive behavior was part of his personality and reputation. The patterns were so routine and so rigid that it detracted from his many positive traits. And the patterns affected those around him. His nervousness triggered our frustration. Whether we were withdrawn or aggressive, everyone was impacted. Each of us responded in our own way. I was not concerned about losing my job so I felt impatient. Others simply avoided interactions.

Through this period, our team consistently achieved and exceeded our targets. We were a leading team within the sales organization. In some ways, John's nervous energy motivated the team to work extra hard so that he didn't feel compelled to interfere with our work. Yet this energy was not sustainable in the long term. There was more nervous energy and the intensity of John's checking-in escalated. Despite significant effort to change the situation, we were not successful. John was fired.

We moved forward, and yet I always wondered if there could have been a better solution. I know his intentions were sincere. I know many people struggle with difficult bosses and many bosses experience distress in their work situation. Toxic relationships, especially involving a boss, are a significant issue in business management.

Our challenge was to calm the situation while maintaining focus on our team goals. From my current experience working with Logosynthesis, this is where I see the benefit of the model: health and productivity. I now recognize an opportunity for a different outcome to this situation. John was regularly triggered by an intense fear of being fired. He could have been coached using Logosynthesis to identify and resolve the frozen perceptions which triggered his frozen reactions. Triggers are held at an energetic level, below our level of cognitive awareness. Although I do not know the exact frozen perceptions, I can recognize areas that could be explored based on patterns of behavior and conversation. One area of blocked energy related to living in a single-income household and having a fear of losing his job. Another area related to an incident at work ten years prior, wherein many sales leaders and his peers were fired for overspending. From his conversations, there also was an experience in his childhood that influenced his reactions. While we recognize that most of us have a fear of losing our jobs, the intensity of his reaction limited his ability to do his job. Applying a cycle of Logosynthesis on the trigger: "I could lose my job." could have offered the first step in helping him feel calmer.

Additionally, I could have worked on my triggers relating

to my responses. My experiences on the farm created a belief that life does not always work out the way we plan but it doesn't stop us from moving forward. Because I did not experience any fear of losing my job, I had difficulty feeling compassionate towards his situation. Logosynthesis could have allowed me to resolve my triggers around my belief that he should act differently.

I did not share his concern about losing a job but my lack of understanding and compassion did not help the situation. I now recognize that by using Logosynthesis, all members on our team could have changed our reactions to create a healthier, more productive work environment.

We did the best we could with the knowledge and resources that were available. I now have a different perspective of the situation. When I shift my programmed responses, I contribute to a more supportive environment. This creates an opportunity for those around me to shift their response. This includes issues as simple as our tone of voice, our choice of words, and our general demeanor. This shift creates a space to have better conversations about challenging decisions, rather than getting stuck in disruptive patterns or simply checking out. This shift supports a more positive culture for our team.

There will always be differences and conflicts on a team. Contrast is vital for learning and growth. When we learn to recognize what bothers us and shift our reactions, we can embrace the differences and be more compassionate towards others. Awareness improves group dynamics. I am now aware of an alternative to firing the boss. I am aware that when I learn to shift how I react in groups, the dynamics of the group shift to create a more supportive environment.

I will share another example. In 2015, I had been asked to take on the role of a volunteer general leader in our local 4-H club. I most certainly did not have the time or the energy to commit to this role. However, due to a sudden vacancy, someone needed to step up.

I used Logosynthesis to help me determine if this was something that was important to me or if I was simply re-acting to a belief that I should help out. I realized that this role was important. I could see how it didn't have to take considerable time and I could shift some other activities in my schedule. I didn't feel the same level of pressure that I had to do it all. I realized that I had the skill set to support leaders and parents, so they could grow in their roles to mentor youth members. In the beginning, I did feel agitated as I rushed home from work and then rushed out the door with my daughters to drive a half hour to attend a meeting. I didn't know everyone so it took time to develop relation-ships. I noticed that when I felt wound up, it impacted how I related to others in the meeting, especially when I did not feel in control of everyone in the room. My daughters were helpful in calling out my patterns of behavior during our drives home. Their feedback highlighted if it felt I was being too forceful in asking a child to present their work or if my tone felt like I was critiquing a member on their work. There was often a disconnect between what I believed and what they perceived. It wasn't always easy for them to offer feedback but I valued the information they provided. I used Logosynthesis to address what bothered me: agitation about being too busy or frustration when things didn't go as planned. I identified the triggers, many relating to being a kid on a busy farm. After each set of sentences, I felt calmer. I didn't feel as agitated leaving work or driving to the meeting. I felt calmer during meetings and I didn't feel the same need to control everything. I was having more fun and it felt like the members, parents, and leaders were having more fun. This created a better space for members to participate and learn. It also created a more positive environment for the adults to feel engaged. Did we run perfect meetings? No, but that was not our goal. Our meetings flowed more smoothly so that we could all learn and have fun. And that was our goal.

Now, five years later, I appreciate that I can use Logosynthesis to resolve other triggers. At times, I benefit from the support of a certified guide. I notice a shift from being stuck in reactive behaviors to feeling in flow with my life. I feel better able to enjoy things that are important to me. And when I feel better, those around me feel better.

I have described how Logosynthesis benefited me during two challenging times in my life. I will also describe how I used Logosynthesis during the initial stages of the global pandemic. During normal times in our household, we purchase groceries every couple of days and enjoy dining out on a regular basis. In the spring of 2020, we were suddenly told to shop for groceries once every two weeks and we were no longer allowed to dine out. This presented a disruption to our normal routine. Had the pandemic occurred before I learned about Logosynthesis, I'm sure that I would have reacted very differently. I would have felt the need to control the meal planning, the shopping list, and the meal preparation. I would not have wanted to do all the work but I am quite certain that I would have felt the need to do it anyway.

So, what happened instead? I noticed that I was able to let my daughter plan out the meals and shopping list. She also cooked delicious meals during this time. I felt calm and patient as I shopped for groceries, wearing my mask and gloves. I really enjoyed our meal time together each evening. We easily sorted out who got to do the dishes. My earlier work with Logosynthesis shifted my patterned responses around being busy to let go of the need to control. I was able to feel calm and relaxed to give space to the rest of my family to do their thing, rather than trying to keep them busy as well.

I recognize that my earlier work with Logosynthesis prepared me for a better experience during the times of the pandemic. While there are many models to support wellbeing, I appreciate the sustained nature of the results when I work with Logosynthesis. The work is not about designing coping strategies to live with what bothers me. The work is about simply noticing what bothers me and using specifically structured sentences to shift the triggers so the issue is resolved. I do not need to cope. I am free to act.

When I free the energy in a trigger, I restore the flow of my creative energy. I recognize that I will encounter many triggers on my path. I am confident that I have access to a simple and powerful method to help me feel better. I can do this on my own or with a guide. I will outline how you can use this book to learn to do the same.

About this book

We will always live in a changing world. However, we have an ability to transform how we react to situations, interact with others, and act in these changing times. This is both our challenge and our opportunity. As individuals, we also have an ability to contribute towards transforming the dynamics of the groups to which we belong. This includes our families, our workplaces, and our communities.

When our life energy is in flow, we feel connected to others and our life has meaning. When we recognize the beautiful simplicity of shifting our focus from changing the world around us to changing our reactions to the world, we begin to notice life begins to flow more smoothly.

When there are sudden changes and uncertainty, we may experience intense feelings. We feel grief when we lose what is important to us. We feel angry when there is injustice. We feel worried when our world is changing rapidly. These responses also provide us with the information to support our healing and development. When we remain stuck in the patterns of grief, anger, and worry, this energy is not available to us. We can use Logosynthesis to restore the flow so that we feel calmer and more focused to take meaningful action. From this position, we create space for those around us to feel better.

In this book, I illustrate how you can use Logosynthesis to help you on an individual basis. You, as an individual, will then be able to create a more supportive environment in your family, your workplace, and your community. When, collectively, we each do our individual work, we recognize a shift in the culture so that we can all engage and thrive.

It is not my ability, desire, or motivation to change you. My purpose in writing this book is to inspire you to begin to use Logosynthesis as a way to let go of what feels distressing and what holds you back in your life. My desire is to help you realize that you are Essence and you have the power to clear the energetic blocks that get in the way of your purpose, even when circumstances feel challenging. You will continue to face challenging situations. You will continue to experience circumstances beyond your control. You will continue to experience loss and change. When you are able to relieve the distressing thoughts, emotions, and body sensations that result, you will be better able to focus on meaningful action.

When we, as individuals, learn to resolve the triggers to our frozen reactions, and thereby shift our automatic responses, we feel better. Our individual responses shift the dynamics of the group. When we collectively shift our individual responses, we influence the culture of our groups and organizations. We are better able to focus on our common goals in a respectful manner. We are better able to quickly adjust to rapidly changing and uncertain external conditions because we are not stuck in the beliefs about how things should be done. We feel more energized and connected through meaningful work.

As you gain an appreciation for what is possible through Logosynthesis, others will notice your energy and will be inspired by your lead. In the next chapter, I illustrate how you can navigate change, as an individual who belongs to families, workplaces, and communities. This is followed by an introduction to the Logosynthesis model. You can use the technique to begin to notice what the shift feels like. A series of illustrations will guide you. To help you appreciate that this is more than a simple technique, I will then share what professional coaches, counselors, and therapists are saying about the model.

Chapter 4 offers case studies provided by professionals trained in Logosynthesis. Their work is presented to demonstrate real life situations, based in different countries, which demonstrate what is possible with Logosynthesis. You may choose to focus on these stories to begin to appreciate how this one method is used to resolve a variety of seemingly unrelated issues.

Much of what bothers us involves layers of experiences, with more than one trigger. As we resolve one layer, we often become aware of another level of the issue. With each cycle of Logosynthesis, we restore the flow of energy. The method is well-suited to self-coaching for many situations. The case studies will help you recognize the benefits of getting support from a trained guide. It is important to reach out for support from a trained professional to resolve deeper issues, such as grief and trauma. You will notice reading the case studies that some issues appear to be resolved in a single session, whereas others are part of a continued theme and supported with a very trusting relationship between the client and guide.

Chapter 5 outlines the pillars of The Healthy Living Plan to help you to thrive in our changing times. This is followed by a guided approach to help you clear your own path to take meaningful action. Suggestions are provided to help you make an impact as an individual within your family, workplace and community.

It is helpful to read the entire book but don't get stuck in trying to understand how Logosynthesis works. Start using the method, guided by the illustrations provided.

Experiment with it. Experience it. Practice it. As you become more familiar with the sentences, you will get into a flow with the process. The theory will begin to make sense. Notice where your thoughts are stuck and apply the method to clear your path. Trust the process. Be curious. Commit to the journey.

It is not important whether you experience an Aha! moment or you notice a gradual shift. This method does not require perfection to begin. It simply requires a curiosity and willingness to explore. The Logosynthesis International Association (LIA) is a valuable resource and further information about LIA is provided in the Appendix under Additional Resources on Logosynthesis.

There are additional books on Logosynthesis that can support your learning. These books are listed in the Appendix. If you work in the healing and guided change professions, I highly recommend that you read *Logosynthesis® Handbook for the Helping Professions* (Lammers, 2015) and *Self Coaching with Logosynthesis®* (Lammers, 2015). Willem has also developed a Logosynthesis Live series to offer further insight into his work. If you are interested in learning how Logosynthesis can support you in everyday life, you can read *Discover Logosynthesis®: The Power of Words in Healing and Development* (Lammers, 2020). Laurie Weiss and myself also write from this perspective.

Throughout the book, I will reinforce the importance of being open to new ideas. Our natural, human tendency when we touch on things that are uncomfortable and distressing is to close in, shut out, and become defensive. At times, our defensive reactions can be quite strong. Some people may discount or dismiss this model because they do not understand how it works. When you notice and resolve your reaction to their response, you create a sense of freedom to explore what is possible. It can be challenging to learn something new when we are busy coping with intense conditions. Yet when we trust the process and have confidence in trying the method, we can begin to notice shifts. It becomes easier to remain open and curious. Magic begins to happen.

CHAPTER 2

Navigating the change

....

*We often cope by changing our conditions,
individually and collectively.
Yet the underlying beliefs and attitudes remain frozen.
We cannot find the space to choose when these
triggers override our cognitive thinking.*

A perspective on change

You can't teach an old dog new tricks. We know it can be hard to break habits and learn new ways of doing things. It can be especially hard when we have been doing them one way for a long time. Yet when our situation suddenly changes, we are forced to learn new tricks. Our ability to adapt requires that we learn how to simply let go of our stuck programming to flow with the changes around us.

In the first chapter, I described how our world can change in an instant and how Logosynthesis can help us thrive during change. In this chapter, I will further explore how we react to change as individuals operating in groups and how Logosynthesis can change our reactions to feel better and improve relationships.

We live in a changing world. If we don't flow with change, we limit our ability to thrive. In some cases, we even limit our ability to survive. We struggle to control what is occurring around us; however, many things are out of our control.

We are human and we react. Our human nature is programmed to respond automatically based on our culture and experiences. When conditions change, our patterns are interrupted. We may feel uncertain, stressed, and scared. We experience distressing thoughts, emotions, and body sensations. When triggered, we respond in an effort to feel better. We cope by changing the situation, by avoiding what makes us feel bad, or by simply doing nothing. These approaches may work for a while but they do not serve us well in the long term. Our creativity, our health, and our relationships suffer.

We are human and we also create. We are better able to thrive when we learn how to let go of our resistance to change. Rather than getting stuck in patterns of complaining about how life should be, we can learn to act according to how life is. Letting go is about freeing our energy that is stuck in reactive patterns so that we are able to think and act in the moment. We are better able to access our creative energy. We are better able to connect with our humanity.

In our everyday lives, we may not always be aware when we are stuck in unhelpful reactive patterns. Yet our body responds by sending signals in the form of distressing thoughts, emotions, and body symptoms. Our thoughts may include: They demand so much from me; I should do more; They should help me; I can't do this. We may experience the emotions of worry, guilt, fear, or anger. Body sensations can feel intense, such as throbbing pain in the chest area, tightness through the core of our body, or heaviness on our shoulders. We often look to change our situation to stop the feelings. Perhaps we accept the situation as unchangeable.

But when we learn to use these responses as information and identify the frozen perceptions that trigger these frozen reactions, the relief can be surprisingly fast.

Logosynthesis helped me during a time of intense change at work. A restructuring resulted in many people losing their jobs. Those of us who remained had to change many of our habits and work routines in a short period of time. I noticed a great deal of intensity in how people reacted. I felt that my brain needed time to process the new information, yet I often felt that I didn't have time to think. It was very easy to get stuck in unproductive conversations with others, such as arguing over the need for more help when additional staff was not an option. I paid attention to what bothered me: I need more help! I connected with the frustration and noticed the feeling in my neck and throat area. As I focused on how I was responding to the workload, I was able to identify a trigger. It was a perception of me, as a child, struggling to keep up with the task of piling bales of hay on the wagon. I applied a cycle of Logosynthesis using the label: 'the perception of piling hay on the wagon'. I noticed a shift and the tension and frustration went away. I no longer was stuck in the pattern of arguing for something that was not going to happen. I was better able to express my concerns, without the same intensity of frustration. I was better able to manage expectations and I felt calmer and more productive. I routinely used the same technique on other issues that bothered me. Over a two-year period of intense change, I used Logosynthesis on a regular basis to prevent getting stuck in unproductive patterns of behavior and to help me feel at ease with my work.

A focus on interaction

Change impacts us as individuals in our groups. We do not live in isolation. We live in families, contribute to workplaces, and participate in communities. These everyday interactions form the complex patterns of our society. We are held together by routines, beliefs, and customs. Although the bonds are not visible to our human eyes, they are very much felt in our human hearts. And they are powerful.

We adopt the beliefs of our groups. When we start to work in a company, we receive formal training on policies and procedures. We also become highly aware of the unwritten rules. When we cross boundaries, we are made aware through reactions, subtle actions, and comments. We know not to repeat the behavior. Often, it is not the words themselves but the energy that is carried with the words that create the impact. I remember a casual conversation with one of my bosses. Suddenly, there was a noticeable shift in tone: "Sometimes I forget who is boss here." There was no mistake that it was a call for me to step down. I had inadvertently crossed a boundary and I knew not to repeat it. The conversation quickly reverted to a light-hearted tone but I got the message and it stayed with me.

Navigating the change

In our families and our communities, we don't have formal job descriptions. We simply know the rules from what we learned as children, what society tells us, and our personal experiences. These patterns contribute to the challenges we experience with gender equity initiatives, cultural differences, and family dynamics. Our interactions are strongly influenced at an energetic level, which operates out of the scope of our cognitive awareness.

The moment we look to introduce change and step beyond the norm, it feels uncomfortable. We might be worried about doing something wrong or being excluded. We might experience a noticeable gut reaction. We might feel that we won't be accepted. We know not to deviate from the norm. The alternative is exclusion and that is threatening.

In many ways, these responses contribute to the survival of the human race. We often speak of adopting change as if we have the power to make a rational choice. Yet we are strongly influenced by our relationships, without even being aware of what is happening. Group interaction is extremely important and very powerful. We may know the written rules yet we *feel* the unwritten rules.

When levels of change and uncertainty are high, our common practice is to introduce new written rules and policies to set expectations. We need to enforce the rules to change and to control the behaviors. Often, we will experience resistance to new rules because they do not match with our habits. We believe the way we used to do things is the right way. Frozen perceptions will trigger frozen reactions. During these times, formal rules are helpful to set expectations, yet there will be unintended violations. Depending on the reprimands for unintended violations, we may experience further resistance to change.

I worked in the food industry so I will provide a hypothetical example related to samples of new items. The marketing group offered free samples to encourage sales staff and customers to try new products. Bruce enjoyed these samples and like his coworkers, he often took any extra home for personal use. One day, senior management changed the policy so that product samples were no longer allowed for employee use. Sales staff still received samples for their customers and they were still interested in trying the new items. Bruce didn't agree with the change in policy because he believed it was important to know what they were selling. Others on his team felt the same way. When Bruce received the samples, he took samples home to try them. A vice president witnessed him leave. Based on the new policy, this was theft. In an effort to demonstrate the seriousness of the initiative, Bruce was fired. He and his coworkers felt the decision was wrong but they were not in a position to change the outcome.

Logosynthesis could help in this situation by coaching employees when there is resistance to new policies. By noticing responses to a policy change, we can locate our triggers and calm our response. We are better able to accept change.

It can help us to embrace new rules. Logosynthesis can also be used by senior management to feel more compassion. When the new rules are broken, they may be better able to engage the employee to determine a creative solution to educate the entire sales team. When we resolve our frozen patterns of reacting, we are better able to adapt to change.

Individuals and change

We've all heard it: Change begins with me.

This statement is both positive and challenging because it means that we own the power to create change. I have enjoyed a long corporate career. I have participated in many annual performance reviews, highlighting strengths and traits that I had to work on. I participated in courses and read books in an effort to change my ways. Yet my personality traits persisted. At times, I was convinced that I was not the one that needed to change. At other times, I worked very hard to change, only to be derailed in the heat of the moment. Despite all my efforts, the characteristics that were flagged early in my corporate career were the same characteristics that were identified in my reviews thirty years later: Cathy can get frustrated when others do not work at her pace.

In a demanding sales environment, this could easily be considered a positive attribute. I knew that the customer always came first. At times, it required a lot of effort throughout the organization to make things happen. In many ways,

I thrived in the male-dominated sales environment. It was normal to have conversations "with tone." I didn't think much of it. From my upbringing, it was normal to experience demanding workloads, which resulted in arguments with my siblings and pushing back on my parents' directions. It felt like a natural part of getting the job done. At work, senior leaders also displayed anger and frustration to get the job done so in many ways, I modeled that behavior.

Then I read *Compelling People: The Hidden Qualities That Make Us Influential* (Neffinger & Kohut, 2013) which noted that women lost influence at work when they got angry. Really? This certainly didn't seem fair. If anger was what was needed to get things done, then I had every right to be angry. But I started to pay attention. I noticed numerous indicators that I was not doing myself any favors when I expressed anger and frustration.

But I still held the belief that it wasn't me that needed to change. I was doing what needed to be done. Others had to change. Systems had to change. I started to really observe that this required a lot of energy and yet nothing changed. In one instance, I was frustrated at work because we used multiple computer systems to forecast product sales, track trade spending, and submit contracts to our customer. The systems were very slow and we had to make a lot of entries. My "hurry up" voice kicked in and when one system was slow, rather than wait for it to respond, I would open another system and start working. My inside voice shouted

Navigating the change

"Hurry up!" I could feel my jaws clench and tightness in my chest. I would complain to my coworkers, who were experiencing the same issues. While we all experienced frustration, I appeared to feel a higher level of intensity than others. Some were able to have engaging conversations while they waited. We were in a regional office so we called the help desk to report the problem. No one in other parts of the country had reported an issue. The process to report the issue took time and I never seemed to get a resolution. I stopped reporting. I continued to be frustrated.

One day, I decided to use Logosynthesis to explore what was happening. I connected with the level of frustration, the thoughts of shouting Hurry up! and the clenching of my jaw and tightness in my chest. This felt intense. I stayed with the feelings and I simply noticed what perceptions came to mind. I was chasing a herd of cows to the barn for milking on a hot, summer day. Cows are notoriously slow on hot days. It didn't matter how loud I shouted 'Hurry Up!' They took their good old time.

I was curious. I said the Logosynthesis sentences using the trigger: The slow cows on a hot day. I allowed time for the words to process. I noticed. The shouting in my head stopped. I was aware of a peaceful walk behind the cows on a beautiful day. I also remembered that we eventually got a border collie to quietly round up the cows, which made my job much easier. The issue didn't last forever and I did what I could at the time.

I reviewed my current situation. I felt calmer waiting for the computer to respond. I called the help desk without getting frustrated. Together with one of my coworkers and the help desk, we discovered an issue that related to a head office backup. It affected the system across the country. It ran during the lunch hour for the staff in our central offices. For those in the other sales offices across the country, they simply didn't think to file a ticket. From a calmer position, we were able to find a solution.

Change is often not comfortable for individuals because it disrupts routines. We look to change our conditions to feel more comfortable. Our opportunity is to simply learn to resolve our triggers to get unstuck and to embrace change. We do this in layers, resolving one issue at a time. We engage the support of coaches or counselors to guide the work, as needed.

When we are able to let go of our programmed responses, we can access our creative energy. From this position, we are better able to flow with the change and uncertainty of our times. We can create a more supportive space for others to do the same.

Groups and change

In our everyday lives, groups operate based on powerful energy dynamics. People express their beliefs as facts. People project tone, emotion, and passion. People influence others using the authority of their position and their connections. In our families, in our workplaces, and in our communities, our response to others influences how they respond to us.

Groups operate based on patterns of behavior and group norms. We are often not even aware of these patterns because they operate at an energetic level. The frozen reactions of individuals in the group result in dynamics that can limit outcomes for the entire group. We think we are making rational, cognitive decisions, yet our decisions are influenced by emotional responses that bypass our cognitive functions. We are not even aware of what is happening. Our frozen reactions are triggered by frozen perceptions based on personal experiences, beliefs, and culture. And the group performance will be influenced by an interaction of individual responses.

In a group dynamic, we form impressions of each individual. We assess this as their character. In Organizational Behavior, we refer to this as Attribution Theory (Heider, 1958). For example, James has called an important meeting after lunch. He knows that everyone is feeling pressure to meet an afternoon deadline, so he wants to respect everyone's time with a punctual start. Anne and Sofia both arrive fifteen minutes late to the meeting. Anne is consistently late for meetings so James feels annoyed when she arrives because, once again, she is disrespectful. Sofia is normally on time so James feels concerned at her late arrival.

James learns that Anne was in a car accident and Sofia simply lost track of time while shopping. He may now feel more empathy for Anne and more annoyed with Sofia. However, he is so conditioned in his response that he simply justifies his initial reaction by attributing Anne's accident to being rushed because she was late anyway. He attributes Sofia's tardiness to other people holding up her up because she is always on time. Although he believes his response is appropriate, he is influenced by previous experiences rather than the current situation. Anne and Sofia will perceive his response and react accordingly. Anne will sense his annoyance and feel that she is not respected. Sofia will sense his acceptance and be reinforced that she did nothing wrong. The group will feel James' response without a rational explanation. They may feel awkward or tense. A pattern in the group dynamic will be reinforced.

In this situation, James is not be able to go back and change his automatic response to the moment. Yet he can use Logosynthesis routinely to interrupt his patterned behaviors. He can explore the late arrivals of Anne and Sofia. He can connect with his thoughts, emotions, and physical sensations in the moment. He can identify triggers and then use the Logosynthesis sentences to gain clarity. This will shift how he automatically responds to both individuals in future incidents.

When James processes his individual reaction to Anne and Sofia, he can reinforce the group rules. Anne and Sofia will recognize their responsibility to the group.

This is an example of an everyday situation in ordinary times. When we are operating in a group that is undergoing a lot of change, team members are already feeling increased pressure. Individuals can be more easily triggered to react inappropriately. The increased intensity creates further tension in the group. The automatic responses are not rational and the dynamics created during the meeting can have longer-term consequences.

We may think that this is an inconsequential example. In my world, people arrive late to meetings all the time. We think that it is no big deal. Yet these are the exact situations that can create patterns of behavior that lead to toxic workplace cultures. When we do not notice and value how we respond in everyday situations, we will be more easily derailed in times of change and uncertainty. In the heat of the moment, Anne may feel that she is always misjudged and quit, leaving a significant skills gap on the team. Someone may make a caustic remark to Sofia because they feel she wasn't held accountable for her behavior. Relationships may suffer. When we are aware of our frozen reactions in these everyday situations, we are better able to address what bothers us during change and uncertainty.

To effectively deal with crisis together—to thrive during intense change and uncertainty—we require a feeling of safety. Each of us has a different tolerance for what feels safe. In normal conditions, we generally understand and follow a common set of rules, both written and unwritten. These rules are generally accepted as fair and there are mechanisms in place to dispute and enforce the rules. At a societal level, we can think of this as being governed by our constitution and our human rights.

Feeling safe reaches beyond physical safety and is influenced by our norms. I will use an example of how our different backgrounds influence not only what we feel but what we notice. Going back to my family norms, we worked hard and we played hard. We didn't think much of a scrape, a sprain, or a bruise. We picked ourselves up and carried on. Fast forward to my role as Executive Director of 4-H Nova Scotia, with a central focus on youth safety and experiential learning. One day, I returned to the office after my parents' 60th anniversary party. My sister had organized a series of outdoor games for the entire family. My siblings and I reverted to our competitive childhood days. My nieces and nephews enthusiastically joined the games. When the injuries occurred, I heard my sister saying: "Just pretend you're not hurt!" The comment didn't register until later. We were operating based on our habitual patterns. The next generation was learning our rules. My brother-in-law and my niece were not injured according to our "rules."

As I returned to the office, I was quite aware of the large gap between what my family viewed as safe and fun and what was required to be safe and fun in this youth organization. I was also aware that because of my norms, I had to pay special attention to this gap. I was at risk of not noticing an incident.

I recognize that the opposite situation also holds true. If I was raised to think that a minor cut is a big deal, I would be programmed to believe that every scrape is an incident. We each have our own experiences to determine what is normal and in a group dynamic we need to respect our different views. We can use Logosynthesis to address what bothers us first, so that we are better able to show respect and have calm discussions when situations do occur.

This example also illustrates how societal norms shift over time. We can see this in many aspects of our lives, especially related to parenting, gender roles, and recognizing ethnic diversity. We are living in a time when the norms and rules are changing very rapidly. We may not be aware of how our frozen perceptions trigger our frozen reactions. We may see nothing wrong with our automatic response yet it may not be acceptable based on current expectations. The new rules may be perceived as unfair. The actions of others may no longer be predictable. Our world feels uncomfortable, and perhaps even threatening. Each of us has a different tolerance for what feels safe and comfortable in the moment. What one person barely notices could trigger panic in another. The level of safety required for the group will depend on the level of discomfort each member experiences in the situation.

As the pace of change increases, the gap between what

an individual requires to feel safe and supported and what the group can provide widens. It can be challenging to be aware of individual feelings around safety. Coping mechanisms kick in. We indicate to others that we are doing fine. We create a shield to feel protected. Yet we may display defensive, aggressive, and bullying behavior. This behavior can trigger a reactive rather than supportive response from others. This is the opposite of what we require. In these conditions, it can be challenging to create a sense of calm in the group. This is where we, as individuals, benefit from noticing what bothers us and using Logosynthesis to shift the energy in our triggers so that we feel better.

Change and uncertainty do not always feel comfortable in our ordinary lives. When we learn to resolve what bothers us, we are better able to feel compassion for what others are experiencing. We are better able to remain calm and enforce necessary boundaries. This creates a space in our groups that feels more supportive for all involved. This is the work that will benefit us immensely as we create a path forward.

Clearing a path forward

Times of rapid change and uncertainty will pass. Yet these times transform our lives forever. The events that occurred during the spring of 2020 have passed. We are motivated to be strong, rebuild what was lost, and create something better than before. Yet the experiences of the onset of the pandemic, the protests, and associated events are frozen in our memories, individually and collectively.

The events will continue to influence our behavior as we move forward. We will notice distressing thoughts, emotions, and body sensations. What we experience will be difficult to rationally explain. Because it doesn't make sense to us, it can feel impossible to explain to others. We may feel angry, sad, or annoyed that life is not fair. We may feel exhausted. We may be stuck in the belief that things should be different. We may simply ignore, dismiss, or avoid the feelings and power through on a new path.

To illustrate how we can clear a path forward, it is beneficial to explore our understanding of how we, as humans, respond to conditions in our everyday lives. The work relates to the following quote:

*Between stimulus and response, there is space.
In that space is our power to choose our response.
In our response lies our growth and our freedom.*

— Viktor E. Frankl / Stephen Covey —

I was first introduced to this quote in *The Seven Habits of Highly Effective People* (Covey, 1989). I loved the idea of choosing my response and I set out to find the space to choose. Throughout my career, I was convinced that I was making great choices and I had evidence to prove it. As

I reflect, I can now observe that many of these "choices" are simply patterns of behavior based on my beliefs, my attitudes, and my experiences. These patterns have served me well.

Work hard. Help others. Stick with it.

Yet I can also observe where these patterns have become rigid and overused. When the world experiences change and uncertainty and my energy is stuck in these patterns, it can be difficult to see other ways of doing things.

I believe that in the space between stimulus and response is the power to choose. Humanity has evolved by finding this space. I also believe that humans have survived by being able to trigger an automatic response that doesn't require space to choose. As humans, we can achieve an automatic response to stimulus from the outside world. These unbelievably quick reactions create our survival instincts. At this level, I believe that there is no space and there is no power to choose. This shows up as deeply embedded beliefs, gut reactions, and emotions. These are the automatic responses that tell us what is "right" and that allow us to live within our families and societies without questioning the facts.

This automatic response to stimulus is what makes us feel comfortable in our everyday living, as we socialize with friends and embrace our work routines. This same automatic response is what triggers anxiety, worry, and fear when we suddenly can't socialize with our friends or our work routines are disrupted. It is what makes some men feel empowered by words and actions that have been unduly celebrated among their peers in homes and workplaces throughout history. The same automatic response triggers confusion, anger, and disbelief when suddenly there are reprimands for the same behaviors.

This automatic response is what makes some women feel fulfilled when caring for others and assuming nurturing roles in their families, workplaces, and communities—and what triggers feelings of being overwhelmed by the belief that they should do it all or that they should do more.

When we suddenly change the rules of our highly programmed operating system, without being aware of the power of these automatic responses, we experience discomfort. Many of these rules have been passed down through our culture over generations. They have played an important role in our ability to thrive as a collective society. We can change the rules at a cognitive level but our body and mind are still programmed to respond in the traditional way at an energetic level. The challenge is that we don't see the energetic structure of this programming so we don't understand the resistance and reactions.

In Logosynthesis terms, we can learn to use our resistance and reactions as information to resolve the frozen perceptions that trigger our frozen reactions. We can work with this information to restore the flow of our energy and to create a path forward.

When conditions in our world are predictable and familiar, life feels normal and comfortable. We know what to do, we do it, and we believe it is the right thing to do. I adopted my patterns from my large, farm family. My parents taught us and modeled behavior based on their own experiences in their large, farm families. We didn't have written job descriptions to define our roles and responsibilities. We intuitively knew what work had to be done. We adopted an efficient, productive way of operating for our situation. For our family, this felt normal and comfortable, despite the arguments about who got to drive the tractors.

As my life progressed, I found myself working and raising my children in a very different environment. I began to notice that my habitual patterns around hard work and helping others created some tension. Referring to the Frankl/Covey quote, I was having difficulty in finding the space between the stimulus and the response. I used mindfulness and yoga to breathe deeply to create a conscious awareness of this space. I tried visualization to see beyond my regular patterns. I focused on exercise and sleep. Yet my patterns persisted and, in the moment, the stimulus triggered a patterned and automatic response. I was not able to find the space to choose.

In the Frankl/Covey quote, the stimulus relates to an event that occurs in the present. From a Logosynthesis perspective, this stimulus can activate a frozen perception

Navigating the change

to trigger a frozen reaction. The frozen perception is an energetic representation of a painful memory, a limiting belief, or wish about how life should be. The trigger creates an intense, automatic response associated with the initial event rather than a response connected to the current situation. The trigger eliminates the space to choose. Using Logosynthesis, we can shift the energy in the trigger to restore the space to choose. This is illustrated as follows:

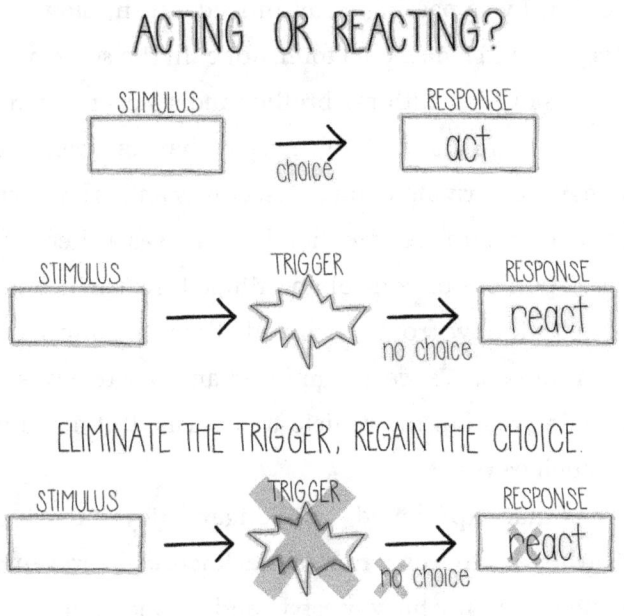

It is helpful to have an appreciation for how these triggers influence our everyday experiences. I live in Canada so I will use a Canadian example. We drive on icy roads. In my city, we often experience not only icy roads but black ice. This is a type of ice you can't even see while you are cruising on the highway.

I have had two car accidents in my life. I consider these to be exceptional events, even though I did not experience physical injuries. Both accidents involved black ice. In the first event, I was passing a car, missed a turn, plowed into a graveyard and smashed a tombstone. In the second situation, I was driving with my brother and sister-in-law in the car. We were on a stretch of highway that was well-known for dangerous driving conditions. It was an early morning in April and I didn't realize that the road was a sheet of ice. The car spun out of control and flipped. As we looked out the front window from our upside-down position, a van crashed into us. We were uninjured and our trip was only slightly delayed but my vehicle was crushed. It could have been much worse.

After that experience, I no longer enjoyed driving on roads when there was a risk of black ice. This presented a challenge given my busy lifestyle and my location. I recognize that because of these two accidents, my winter driving experience is very different from those around me.

Consider the following scenarios to recognize how we

can have very different experiences driving on the same roads in the winter:

- Ellen hasn't had an accident nor has she experienced any issues with black ice. When she drives in winter conditions, she knows to be cautious because she has been educated on driving in winter weather. She does not feel especially tense while driving because she has no experience of an accident. She feels confident in her driving.

- Vicki experienced an accident on black ice but she was not injured. She knew it could have been worse. When she heads out in wintery weather, she experiences tension in her neck and shoulders because she knows what can happen. She grips the steering wheel tighter than normal because she is cautious. She feels triggered and she often does not go out if she doesn't need to. She is fine but on edge.

- Vicki now drives her daughters to their activities on winter evenings. They sit beside her and they can feel her tension. She feels more nervous than when driving on her own because she is risking their safety as well. Her daughters pick up on these feelings. They want to play their music to relax but Vicki wants to keep things quiet so she can better focus on the road ahead.

- Vanessa has experienced a serious accident on black ice, through no fault of her own. She suffered a broken leg and a back injury. Now she experiences an intense fear that something may happen again. This frozen reaction is so strong that she does not feel able to drive in icy conditions.

With this perspective, we can begin to appreciate how our current experience is influenced by past events. We can also recognize that others experience the same current conditions differently from us and how those around us will react to our response.

I have been able to use Logosynthesis to calm my reactions to winter driving. I connected to the feelings of tension and the thoughts about what could have happened. I was able to identify triggers from the accident, such as the car spinning out of control, the image of seeing the van hit our car, and my sister-in-law's leg pushing snow away from the back window. After using Logosynthesis, I know there are other winter-driving triggers yet I now feel calmer when driving in these conditions.

As we look to clear our path forward, it helps to remember that we all are human and we all react to what life throws our way. We are all in the same storm yet we are on very different ships. We have individual and collective experiences. While we may not be able to calm the storm, we can learn to feel calm in the storm. When we feel calm, those around us are better able to feel calm. We are also better able to access resources and work together to improve the experience for all involved.

We know that our world can change in an instant and it will not always feel comfortable. We will navigate change as individuals through our interactions in our families, workplaces, and communities. We benefit if we can clear our triggers to create the space between the stimulus and the response to choose to act.

In the next chapter, I show you how Logosynthesis works, step by step. I will then provide a variety of case studies to help you recognize how this one method can help you thrive in your everyday life. I will also outline how this model supports healthy living and offer a guide to help you to shift your reactions to action to clear your path forward to enjoy life.

CHAPTER 3

Introducing Logosynthesis

The simplicity and power of Willem's work in the development of Logosynthesis lies in two foundational questions:
- *What is your mission in this life?*
- *What gets in the way of this mission?*

How Logosynthesis works

*Logosynthesis is a model for
self-coaching and guided change
based on the power of words and sentences
to change energy fields.*

— Dr. Willem Lammers —

In the first two chapters of this book, I identified how our world can suddenly change and how this can feel uncomfortable, even painful. I described how our automatic and patterned responses kick in when we are faced with change and uncertainty. I indicated how Logosynthesis can help to create our path forward. In this chapter, you will learn to use the model. The illustrations offer a guide to help you get comfortable using the method on a regular basis. I will then provide case studies to illustrate how this model is being used to achieve sustained relief for a wide variety of issues.

Using the principles of the Logosynthesis model, in Chapter 5 I will describe the pillars of The Healthy Living Plan and offer a guide to resolve what bothers you to clear your path for action.

I will begin here by outlining the foundation of the model so you can better understand how it delivers such remarkable results.

Logosynthesis is a model with a philosophy, a theory, an attitude, and specific methods. It is anchored in two foundational questions:

1. What is your mission in this life?
2. What gets in the way of this mission?

Taking time to reflect on what gives meaning to our lives is an important first step in helping us thrive. The second question allows us to recognize where we can focus our attention to resolve blocks and barriers. We can recognize where our energy is frozen in our painful memories, limiting beliefs, and ideas about how our life should be. When we gain awareness of both what is meaningful and what gets in the way, we can begin to resolve the blocks and take action.

The philosophy of Logosynthesis can be summarized as follows:

Introducing Logosynthesis

> *We are Essence - life energy with a life purpose.*
> *Essence is energy in flow and does not suffer.*
> *Suffering occurs when we lose connection with Essence.*
> *Energy is frozen or in flow.*
> *Energy is in the right or wrong place.*
> *Energy belongs to us or it doesn't.*
> *Words have the power to shift energy.*
>
> — Dr. Willem Lammers —

We gain an appreciation for the significance of these principles with practice and training. Anyone who has experienced one of Willem's seminars can begin to appreciate that these foundational principles have a profound impact on our life experience. The beauty of the Logosynthesis model is that Willem has developed a Basic Procedure so that we can restore the flow of Essence to relieve distress, even if we don't understand the theory behind the principles. Each one of us is Essence and the principles hold true, regardless of our situation. Willem offers an introduction to his work in his latest book, *Discover Logosynthesis®: The Power of Words in Healing and Development*.

Logosynthesis was developed as a model for healing and development in the field of trauma and anxiety. There are many methods to support healing and development. There are many techniques and tips to help us manage stress and anxiety. There are well-recognized ways to get our energy flowing. To my knowledge, Logosynthesis is unique in its ability to target distressing thoughts, emotions, and body sensations to offer relief. Using the energetic power of words and specific sentences, we can resolve the frozen perceptions that trigger frozen reactions. This shift from coping with distress to resolving distress is transformational. The shift occurs at an energetic or spiritual level, creating results that are not possible at a physical or mental level.

Willem describes the literal meaning of Logosynthesis as "using words to put people back together." His work is inspired by great minds in psychotherapy, psychology, philosophy, and spirituality. He refers to the phrase: We stand on the shoulders of giants. He has learned from many great thought leaders to further our understanding in the field of healing and development.

The name Logosynthesis derives from Viktor Frankl's work in Logotherapy and Roberto Assagioli's work in Psychosynthesis. Willem's extensive experience with Transactional Analysis (TA) and Neurolinguistic Programming (NLP) have provided a foundation for his own work. His experience with various forms of energy psychology to treat Post Traumatic Stress Disorder (PTSD) recognizes the important influence of subtle energy. Logosynthesis also references many spiritual teachings across religions and throughout history which affirm that we, as humans, are more than body and mind. These spiritual teachings also recognize that words have an energy which holds a power to create our reality. In addition to this background, for many years, Willem led the Institute for Applied Social Sciences, a leading Swiss training institute for work-related counseling.

Willem recognizes that all models of guided change are rooted in the culture and societies of the developer. Logosynthesis is rooted in Western society and culture at the beginning of the 21st century. Willem is a Dutch-Swiss psychologist. I think he is an *echte Hollander*, a real Dutchman. His work is precise, intuitive, and rich with academic intellect and practical experience. The Logosynthesis model is based on a structured protocol. The sentences have been crafted, with specific words selected, so that we do not need to understand the background theory. Our Essence knows and understands the meaning of the words. We simply need to trust that this process works. As we become more comfortable with the method, we are better able to quiet our mind and allow the process to happen. We can reach a deeper level of connection and flow.

Logosynthesis offers a model that recognizes the power of Essence, our life energy. We may know this energy as our higher Self or our immortal soul. Around the globe and throughout the generations, humans have created language and forms of expression to connect with their Essence. The expression is always relative to the knowledge and culture of the time. Much of what we know of Essence has been shared through stories. We have survived and thrived as a race by learning how to connect with this energy, both individually and collectively. We have learned to nurture this connection through activities such as prayer, music, song, meditation, and rituals.

In our fact-based world, this expression can struggle to have a voice amid the demands for scientific evidence. In our global society, we struggle to recognize the similarities among various forms of expression. In the steady stream of external media, facts, and data, we can have difficulty hearing our powerful inner voice. We may listen to the voices of authority at the expense of this inner voice, rather than nurturing both perspectives. Our outward expressions, based on our language, culture, and religion, can be either challenged or celebrated. In recognizing our Essence, we can universally connect beyond our differences. This is the level of the work of Logosynthesis. At this level, we feel meaning in our lives and we can thrive through times of change and uncertainty.

Logosynthesis provides a model that allows us to recognize what bothers us through the lens of Essence. Here we are able to tap in to one simple solution for what our mind perceives as many different problems. Distressing thoughts. Negative emotions. Painful body sensations. Our thoughts, emotions, and sensations do not reside in our body or our mind. They are frozen energy residing in our personal space (see Appendix for a definition of this term). When we approach healing and development from the level of energy, the results are surprising.

Based on this understanding, our task in relieving what bothers us is to restore the flow of our life energy. Willem has developed very specific sentences to shift the energy bound in the frozen perception (X) to relieve our suffering. The specific sentences are:

- *I retrieve all my energy bound up in this (X) and take it to the right place in my Self.*
- Working pause. (A pause to let the words work)
- *I remove all non-me energy related to this (X) from all of my cells, all of my body and my personal space, and send it to where it truly belongs.*
- Working pause.
- *I retrieve all of my energy bound up in all of my reactions to this (X) and take it to the right place in my Self.*
- Working pause.

We may be curious about the nature and meaning of the three sentences. Willem reminds us that words have power to manifest beyond their meaning. Words focus the speaker's intention and will to create. In spiritual traditions, the power of words is the origin of creation.

The specific words used in the Logosynthesis sentences are designed to restore our energy flow. The sentences shift the energy that is stuck in the trigger. The working pause between each sentence allows time for the energy to shift. The amount of time required can vary depending on the intensity of the memory, belief, or fantasy. There is generally a feeling of calm and clarity after the words process. This graphic helps to illustrate what is happening during the simple yet powerful process:

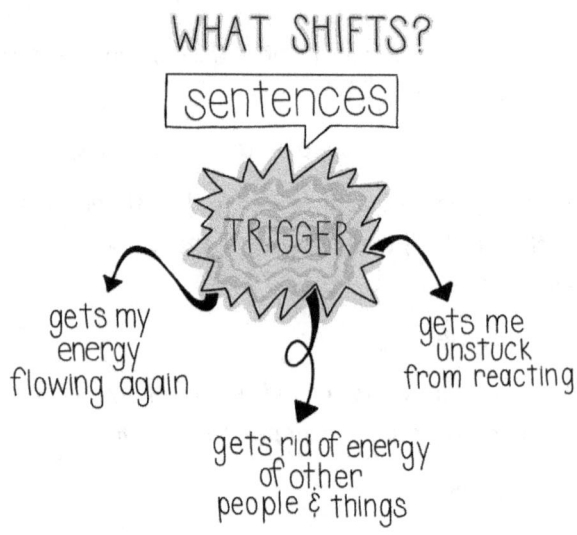

Willem helps us to understand this energetic and spiritual model through the use of metaphors and measures. By measuring the level of distress before and after the application of the sentences, we can understand something that we cannot see. The rating is based on Subjective Units of Distress Scale (SUDS), which is a standard measurement in psychology. It is used to quantify emotions based on a self-assessment scale from 0 to 10, with 0 being no distress and 10 being the most distressing possible. It measures the subjective intensity of distress currently experienced by the individual.

Logosynthesis works to relieve distress. Our distress, by definition, is not a comfortable topic to explore and this process therefore often requires a trusting relationship with a coach, counselor, or therapist. While the structure supports both the guide and the client when working in guided change, the Logosynthesis method also creates safety and trust when we are self-coaching.

When we experience events in our lives, we freeze our energy in structures that I have described earlier as triggers. When these triggers are activated, we experience distress. As humans, we have created defensive patterns to avoid feeling this discomfort and pain. We layer more frozen perceptions which trigger frozen reactions. We get angry to avoid feelings of abandonment. We may be driven to overachieve to mask low self-esteem. As we gain confidence using the Logosynthesis method, we trust that we can peel away the layers to feel more peace, calm, and clarity. We are then better able to thrive by connecting with our true Self.

The speed and simplicity of this specific method may lead us to think of Logosynthesis as merely a tool. It is not. We do not need to understand all of the theory to apply the methods but we do need to appreciate that the process is anchored in a compassionate philosophy. In the beginning, you may be tempted to make changes to the simple method or the words. I have learned to trust that Willem has created the model based on a career supporting healing and development and I trust his selection of words to offer relief. I have also learned that as we become comfortable and establish a flow using the method, we experience deeper results.

Willem likens this to learning the notes to create the music. Like any instrument, we shift from playing the notes to creating music through consistent practice of the basic notes. The results are amplified through coaching and training.

For many people I work with, it is their first time experiencing the kind of shift that occurs during Logosynthesis. There is often a degree of bewilderment and curiosity about what happened. Something has changed but they are not sure how it happened. They only have their individual experience but they do not have the perspective of others who have used Logosynthesis. Having worked with the method for over five years, I notice very consistent results:

Presenting issue.

Intervention.

Presenting issue resolved.

My guidance for people when they are first introduced to the work is simply to trust the process. The method is structured so that you don't need to understand *how* it works for it to work. You can simply follow the steps and practice.

As with any type of work, asking for help and support from someone trained in the model will enhance your results. I also know from my many conversations, there can be resistance to the process because it is a new and different approach. This is a normal response to something new and different. We learn through experience. I encourage you to be curious and to continue learning.

Learning to use the Basic Procedure

Logosynthesis works by applying the same simple technique over and over. As we become more comfortable with using the method, the work flows more smoothly and we can resolve deeper levels of distress. In the beginning, we may not be comfortable with allowing what bothers us to surface. When we become comfortable with the technique and the results, we learn to trust that the specific words used in Logosynthesis make the feelings go away.

Logosynthesis offers a gentle and compassionate process. When we know that we only have to be with the feelings for a short while to eliminate the trigger, it is easier to follow the process. It is in the working pause between the sentences that the energy shifts and the issues fall away. For more distressing issues, we allow a longer working pause between the sentences. I have provided a video of the guided process on The Healthy Living Plan YouTube channel (see Appendix) to demonstrate the technique.

The steps of the Basic Procedure for Logosynthesis include:

1. **THE PREP:** Get comfortable before you start, whether on your own or with a trained professional.

2. **THE DISTRESS:** Notice what bothers you. These are frozen reactions in the form of distressing thoughts, emotions, and body sensations. Rate the level of distress on a scale from 0-10.

3. **THE TRIGGER:** Allow any images, sounds, or other sensory perceptions to surface. The frozen perception is always perceived as one of the five sensory perceptions: sight, sound, touch, taste or smell. Label this trigger.

4. **THE SENTENCES:** Apply the three specific Logosynthesis sentences to the trigger, allowing working pauses for the words to process. The sentences are:

    - *I retrieve all my energy bound up in this (trigger) and take it to the right place in my Self.*

    - *I remove all non-me energy related to this (trigger) from all of my cells, all of my body and my personal space, and send it to where it truly belongs.*

    - *I retrieve all of my energy bound up in all of my reactions to this (trigger) and take it to the right place in my Self.*

5. **THE ASSESSMENT:** Reassess what bothers you and rate the current level of distress on the SUDS scale. Repeat the cycle as issues arise.

That's it! The specific sentences shift the energy in the frozen perceptions. When the frozen perception shifts, it no longer triggers the distressing frozen reactions.

Using the following illustrated guide, you can try it now or set aside time later to practice the technique. You can use these graphics to guide your learning and to begin practicing the Basic Procedure on your own. Remember that we are encouraging progress, not perfection. We encourage you to be curious to explore what may feel uncomfortable in the beginning. As you use the pictures to guide the process, you will gain a deeper understanding of and appreciation for the process.

the prep
BEFORE YOU BEGIN.

 RELAX

GET A GLASS OF WATER

NO INTERRUPTIONS

BE CURIOUS

don't worry about being perfect!

GIVE IT A TRY!

Introducing Logosynthesis

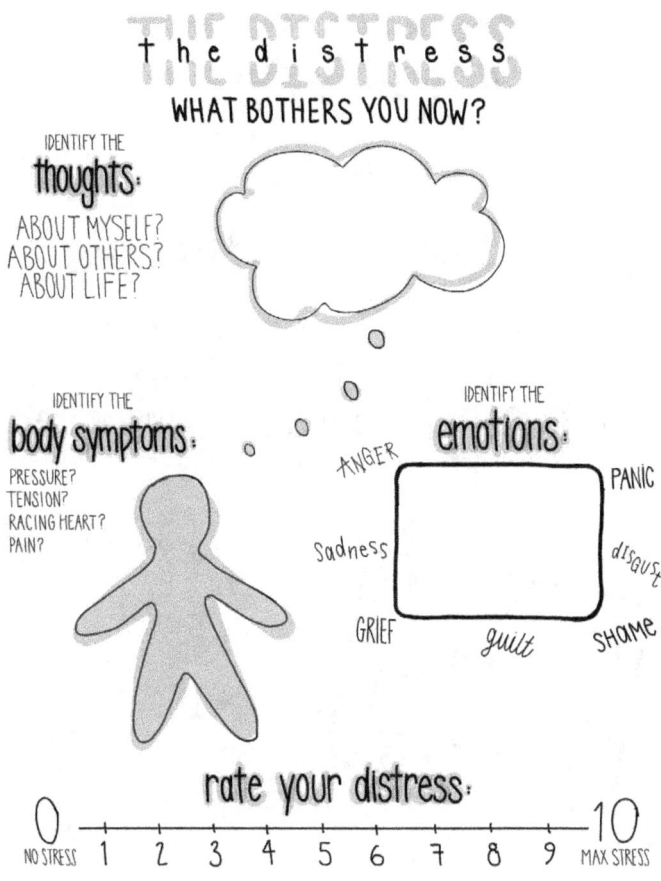

the trigger
WHAT DO YOU OBSERVE?

WHAT...

do i see?
PERSON, OBJECT, SCENE?
COLOR, SIZE, MOVEMENT?
SHAPE?

do i hear?
VOICES, NOISE, MUSIC?
VOLUME, PITCH?
OTHER?

do i sense in the space around or within me?
TEMPERATURE? PRESSURE? VIBRATION? SKIN CONTACT? OTHER?

do i perceive?
LOCATION
LEFT RIGHT
↑FRONT BACK↓
DISTANCE?

HELLO, MY TRIGGER IS...

WHAT DO YOU NOTICE?
label the trigger

Introducing Logosynthesis

the sentences
ELIMINATE THE TRIGGER.

▶ **PLAY** — I RETREIVE ALL OF MY ENERGY BOUND UP IN [HELLO, MY TRIGGER IS ____], AND TAKE IT TO THE RIGHT PLACE IN MY SELF.

⏸ PAUSE
allow the words to work

▶ **PLAY** — I REMOVE ALL NON-ME ENERGY RELATED TO [HELLO, MY TRIGGER IS ____] FROM ALL OF MY CELLS, ALL OF MY BODY AND MY PERSONAL SPACE, AND SEND IT TO WHEREVER IT TRULY BELONGS.

⏸ PAUSE
allow the words to work

▶ **PLAY** — I RETRIEVE ALL OF MY ENERGY BOUND UP IN ALL MY REACTIONS TO [HELLO, MY TRIGGER IS ____], AND TAKE IT TO THE RIGHT PLACE IN MY SELF.

⏸ PAUSE
allow the words to work

the assesment
WHAT DO YOU NOTICE NOW?

WHAT CHANGES DO YOU NOTICE IN WHAT BOTHERS YOU?

WHAT CHANGES DO YOU NOTICE IN THE TRIGGER?

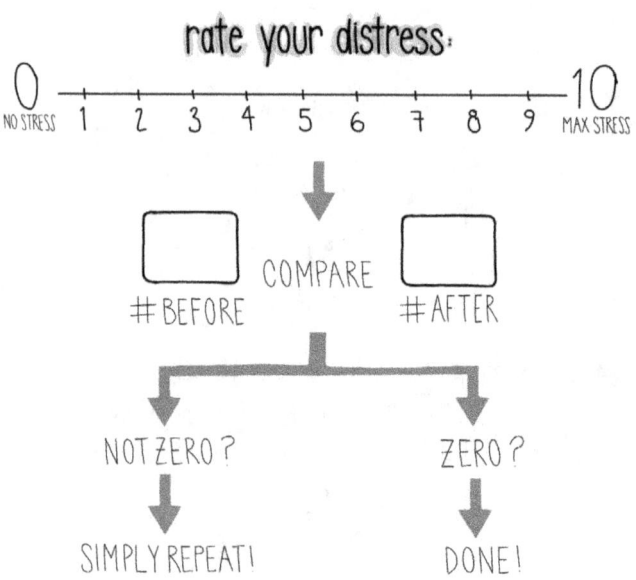

The Empty Chair exercise

In everyday life, we interact with and react to other people. At times, these interactions and reactions may feel intense and distressing. The words and behaviors of other people may bother us. How we respond to each other impacts our relationships. When working with the Logosynthesis model, we can learn to use our responses as information and process what bothers us. This improves our relationships and group dynamics. It can be difficult to imagine how our feelings towards another person might change, especially if we have been stuck in the pattern for a while. It is helpful to experience what shifts through a guided exercise.

The Empty Chair exercise is a technique used in the Logosynthesis® Basic Training course. A video, guided by Willem, is also available on The Healthy Living Plan YouTube channel. The goal of this exercise is to simply notice how your feelings towards another individual shift after the exercise.

To start, think of someone who has mildly annoyed or irritated you and place the person in an imaginary chair. This is not an exercise in thinking of a highly emotional relationship. It is meant to allow you to notice your subtle energy, often felt through the core of your body. For most of us, this takes some guidance because we have been conditioned to avoid these feelings. However, this is a necessary first step in the process. Energy shifts may feel intense.

I advise that you become familiar with the technique on milder issues and seek the guidance of a Practitioner in Logosynthesis® for support with more intense feelings.

We can experiment with the steps as follows:

- Relax and focus on your breathing.
- Imagine an empty chair.
- Imagine a person in this chair who mildly annoys or irritates you, for whatever reason. Connect with the thoughts, emotions and physical sensations.
- Measure the level of distress on a scale of 0–10. This will be your SUDS rating.
- Apply the Logosynthesis sentences:
- *I retrieve all my energy bound up in the "representation of the person sitting in the chair" and take it to the right place in my Self.*
- Working pause.
- *I remove all non-me energy related to the "representation of the person sitting in the chair" from all of my cells, all of my body and my personal space, and send it to where it truly belongs.*
- Working pause.
- *I retrieve all of my energy bound up in all of my reactions to the "representation of the person sitting in the chair" and take it to the right place in my Self.*
- Working pause.
- Now assess your emotions, body sensations, or thoughts

toward this person on a SUDS scale of 0–10.
- What has shifted or changed?

Remember that curiosity is powerful! Pay attention to how you interact with this person the next time you meet.

Learning what professionals are saying

I am not a psychologist, counselor, or psychotherapist and so it is important to me that I understand the benefits of Logosynthesis as compared to other methods used for anxiety, depression, anger management, and other issues. As President of The Healthy Living Plan Inc., I have conducted several surveys among an international Facebook group consisting of professional coaches, counselors and therapists with various levels of training in Logosynthesis.

In a November 2017 survey, respondents indicated that Logosynthesis was their preferred method to work with clients presenting with issues that include anxiety, depression, PTSD, burnout, loss, abuse, anger management, and others. Respondents cited benefits that include overall effectiveness, speed of work, ease of use, client comfort, and that Logosynthesis targets presented issues.

Cognitive Behavior Therapy (CBT) is a leading psychotherapy model used to support individuals with mental health concerns, such as anxiety, depression, PTSD, and others. In November 2018, I surveyed individuals in the

Logosynthesis Facebook group who have training in both Logosynthesis and CBT. I asked respondents to provide commentary from their experience working with clients to highlight which was their preferred method and why. Most respondents expressed a clear preference for Logosynthesis. Here is a sample of what they said:

- *Logosynthesis, since it is much faster, more sustainable and easier to use.*

- *I believe, from my experience, that Logosynthesis is more comprehensive than CBT, because it addresses physical symptoms and emotions as well as cognitive behaviors. Logosynthesis offers a simple holistic approach to suffering.*

- *Logosynthesis is the preferred model as it effectively dissolves the triggers and therefore the distress the client seeks assistance for. It is a simple process for the therapist to apply and it is gentle on the client's system when re-processing the material (especially for clients with trauma, which is the typical issue / population I treat).*

- *CBT manages all the symptoms, feelings, and reactions so it can be only superficial. Logosynthesis resolves the triggers, thus enabling a profound shift in oneself.*

- *Logosynthesis is my preferred choice as I find it more efficient and clients love how quick it works and that they can do it easily at home once they have experienced it.*

- *It is easier with Logosynthesis. After the surprise effect, clients adhere to the model and ask to use it themselves after a few sessions.*

- *Logosynthesis reaches much deeper levels of transformation. It effects the emotional and the spiritual level. And my clients can easily do self-coaching with Logosynthesis.*

In January 2020, I asked questions of the same Facebook group to better understand the impact of Logosynthesis on their professional self-care and for working with clients. Of the 35 respondents with various levels of training, 83% indicated that Logosynthesis has transformed their approach as a coach, therapist, or guide. One respondent indicated: "I no longer beat around the bushes but focus on what matters and achieve results. I make better usage of time: I no longer focus on having my clients discover and practice behaviors or techniques, nor do they spend countless hours to practice such new behaviors in order to counteract their inner problem. They just solve the problem and move on, thus reducing effort, time, and energy for both of us, client & coach."

In the same survey, 79% of respondents said that they use Logosynthesis on a daily or weekly basis for their own professional self-care. Further, 89% rated Logosynthesis as either highly preferred or preferred compared to other available models for professional self-care. They provided these comments:

- *The reason is simple: more effective!*
- *I find it very flexible and can use it for many issues.*
- *It is the most effective model of them all. I can go deep fast*

with Logosynthesis, solve the problem (not just talk about it), and achieve long-lasting change without relapse.

- *An easy, effective, fast model for change when breathing doesn't work.*
- *It helps release any reactions that I have in the present, helps to identify other layers in my past, and connects me to my Essence while keeping me grounded in the world we reside in.*

Additionally, 80% of respondents indicated that Logosynthesis is their preferred model to work with clients. Their comments include:

- *No bullshit.*
- *It allows deep change in a relatively short time and clients respond well, especially after getting more familiar with it.*
- *Because of its effectiveness and speed, it sits alongside my coaching work when I use other models too. Some clients are ready for Logosynthesis and some not so much.*
- *I get great results with it. People are hungry for results. Once they try it, they're sold.*
- *It's my preferred model to use to work with trauma and distressing experiences.*
- *Different clients have different needs. Some need more consultation and guidance. When there is a need for transformational work, I almost always choose Logosynthesis.*
- *Easy, fast, healing, helpful: They can learn how to use it in self-coaching.*

New discoveries can require time to gain acceptance

and understanding. When our usual methods of coping no longer meet our needs, we have an opportunity to use Logosynthesis to support our ability to thrive. With a focus on healthy living, I now recommend Logosynthesis to feel better. The reason is simple. Logosynthesis is fast and easy to use. Logosynthesis costs nothing to use. Logosynthesis resolves what bothers us, regardless of the issue. And the more we use it, the more comfortable it feels.

I have described what Logosynthesis is and how you can start to use the method. I have provided some theory to help you appreciate how Logosynthesis can offer such powerful results. I have shared feedback from professional coaches, counselors, and therapists trained in the method so you can understand why this model is their preferred method for their own professional self-care and for working with clients. The next chapter offers a series of case studies to demonstrate how coaches, counselors, and therapists work with Logosynthesis. You will see how one fast and easy method can resolve a variety of issues and help you to thrive in our times.

CHAPTER 4

Logosynthesis in action

....

*Logosynthesis offers one
simple and powerful method
to provide relief for issues
which may appear to be unrelated.
This is the power of Essence.*

Sharing our stories

In this section, I present a series of case studies that have been written by an international group of professional coaches, counselors, and therapists trained in Logosynthesis. They have offered an example of their work to demonstrate how they use Logosynthesis to support their clients. The names in the case studies have been changed. The topics illustrate how one method can offer relief and support in a variety of situations, which may appear to be unrelated. Some stories relate to the distress created directly from an exceptional global event: the Covid-19 pandemic. Other stories relate to challenges and exceptional events in an individual's life. The common theme in the case studies is that an individual was seeking professional support for relief from an issue that bothered them. In all cases, Logosynthesis was used and the individual reported feeling better after the session.

LOGOSYNTHESIS IN ACTION

- BURNOUT
- panic attacks
- DISTRESS
- grief
- FEAR
- frustration
- CONFIDENCE
- calm + focused

The case studies illustrate that the client does not need to understand the theory behind Logosynthesis in order to experience the results. Willem has developed the specific sentences, recognizing the power of Essence and of words, to do the work from a higher level of consciousness. You will notice that when the client identifies the trigger, simply saying the Logosynthesis sentences with working pauses will shift the energy to relieve the distress. The client feels better after saying the sentences.

The case studies vary in length because, in some cases, the presenting issue is resolved after one cycle of Logosynthesis. In other cases, the processing that occurs may activate another issue. The method is simply repeated until the guide and client feel comfortable wrapping up the session. The skill and training of the guide will offer support for the client. Processing can continue after the session, so the guide plays an important role in supporting the client for deeper issues. Practitioners in Logosynthesis® vary in the range of issues they will address with clients within the parameters of their professional training as coaches, counselors, and therapists.

The case studies provided below highlight that, although we may not be able to change our situation, we can change how we react to our situation. We can resolve what bothers us to feel better and to gain clarity to move forward. We can learn to enjoy the flow of extraordinary living.

Case Study 1: Overcoming fear

At times, our responses in everyday situations can feel intense. The actions of others may not meet our expectations and we suffer. Logosynthesis offers a fast and easy guided approach to resolve the triggers so we can feel calm and confident to make the most of the situation.

Case Study provided and written by: Alan Rojas-Yacolca
Certification: Logosynthesis® Trainee
Role: Energy Healer, Developmental Educator & Coach
Website: www.alanry.com
Location: Lima, Peru

Dina is a psychologist and humanistic psychotherapy trainee in her mid-40s. Recently, she attended a complimentary online webinar I hosted on relieving stress using Logosynthesis. We both reside in Lima, Peru. During the beginning minutes of our online coaching session, it became quite clear for both of us that she was feeling moved by what has been happening over recent weeks: the global health crisis caused by the Covid-19 pandemic; the behaviors she perceives in others, both on social media and in the community where she lives; the possibility of contagion; and the fear of what may happen in the future. For me, these issues appear to be a recurrent pattern lately on social media and in my conversations as a coach.

I asked Dina what she seeks in our coaching session.

She described a situation where she had to visit a bank to cash an emergency aid check issued by the government. While waiting in line, she heard someone coughing right behind her. When she turned around, she discovered this person was not wearing his mask appropriately. Dina was startled. The person then clarified that his cough was due to a seasonal allergy. She explained to me: "All the same, the risk is always there. I was tired of seeing people not observing precautions. They should observe social distance and safety measures!"

I asked her to rate her distress from 0 to 10, with 10 being the most distressing. She offered a SUDS rating of 8 or 9.

Together we mapped what was happening to cause her suffering. She noticed the memory of standing in line at the bank and listening to the person cough and seeing him not wearing a mask appropriately. She then noticed videos on Facebook where others were not observing social distance as they should. She felt angry. She received messages on her WhatsApp family group with daily news on how many people are infected and videos of accumulated corpses in black plastic bags at a local hospital.

During the session, Dina told me: "The system is about to collapse, that's scary. At times I still catch myself spacing out, blanking, or I'm too distracted to concentrate on writing reports for my job." This whole thing is wearing me out. It's as if this was all over me, I feel suffocated. I've come to this session to find relief and to stop feeling so insecure."

Dina has no siblings. Both of her parents are elderly and depend on her. As she told me: "It's essential for me to take good care of myself now to protect them from contagion. Likewise, as I now work from home, I need to do things right. I need to be focused now. I must concentrate or I could lose my job. I cannot afford that."

Dina's energy was stuck in several stress-provoking situations all at one time. It was understandable that she could not focus. To help her focus and find relief, we started by sensing where the most tension was accumulated. She replied: "In anger. I'm angry all the time about others, especially those who do not obey rules. It's because of them that others like me could get infected. They are so selfish!"

She felt this anger in her clenched jaw and stiff hands. She also noticed a lump in her throat. She provided a SUDS rating of 8.

I asked her to notice what perceptions arise. Several scenes came to her mind: the scene at the bank; the social media videos portraying people not respecting quarantine rule; the dead people. While reviewing those scenes she realized that the theme is consistent. She has an expectation that "others should always obey quarantine rules…or else."

We labeled this expectation as the trigger. She closed her eyes and followed my lead in a cycle of Logosynthesis:

- *I retrieve all my energy bound up in this "expectation that others should always obey quarantine rules…or else" and take it to the right place in my Self.*

Logosynthesis in action

- Working pause.
- *I remove all non-me energy related to this "expectation that others should always obey quarantine rules...or else" from all of my cells, all of my body and my personal space, and send it to where it truly belongs.*
- Working pause.
- *I retrieve all of my energy bound up in all of my reactions to this "expectation that others should always obey quarantine rules...or else" and take it to the right place in my Self.*
- Working pause.

She took her time and let the phrases do the work. After a few minutes, she sighed. The processing was over. Dina appeared to be a bit more relaxed. She now offered a SUDS rating of 6 out of 10. I asked what kept her stress at a 6. The look on her face changed. She claimed to be scared now. "What if I get infected?" She looked down in silence.

I asked: "What's going on now that you're looking down?"

She paused and replied: "My parents. I... I don't want to lose them." She admitted that losing them had been her worst nightmare for a long time. The pandemic seemed to make it even more possible than before. Tears rolled down her face. "I'm scared of getting infected and infecting them."

Her SUDS rating was now 8.

She explained she has been scared of them dying since she was eight years old. At the time, both her parents were in a car accident. It was not serious but she got scared. She thought they could die. Now, during the session, she pictured herself lonely and abandoned. In her mind's eye, Dina had a picture of herself as an 8-year-old child, at home and alone at night, with no one there to share a meal with her anymore.

We labeled this as the trigger and applied another cycle of Logosynthesis:

- *I retrieve all my energy bound up in this "scene of being 8, at home and alone at night, and everything it represents" and take it to the right place in my Self.*
- Working pause.
- *I remove all non-me energy related to this "scene of being 8, at home and alone at night, and everything it represents" from all of my cells, all of my body and my personal space, and send it to where it truly belongs.*
- Working pause.
- *I retrieve all of my energy bound up in all of my reactions to this "scene of being 8, at home and alone at night, and everything it represents" and take it to the right place in my Self.*
- Working pause.

The working pauses took longer than before. The initial tears yielded to a deep sigh. Her stooped posture was now upright. She inhaled and exhaled deeply. She opened her eyes and sipped some water and paused. She blinked repeatedly and appeared to be still processing. I observed rapid eye movements. I waited.

Dina then sighed and said: "I will not be alone. I am an adult now. I can take charge of myself. Besides, I have a family: my cousins. We get along and see each other from time to time. My parents are healthy now and they are also obeying the rules. I'm being careful."

She now gave a SUDS rating of 2.

It was then time to assess our work in this session and examine what had changed or if there was anything left to process. Dina felt that the behavior of others was not important. She felt she could skip Facebook. She felt she could ask her relatives to stop sending videos or simply avoid watching them. The scene at the bank no longer bothered her.

At the beginning of the session, Dina's confidence was rated as a 46 on a self-assessed, subjective scale of 1 to 100. By the end of the session, it was 90. Her distress level, provided as a SUDS rating, had moved from 8 to 2 or 1. She was again feeling relaxed and confident.

Two weeks later, I received a quick message from Dina. Her confidence remained the same. She was much calmer and she was able to better concentrate at work. Both her parents were healthy. She shared that she was again enjoying her favorite hobby: reading.

Case Study 2: Creating willingness

It is natural for a parent to want to relieve a child's distress around everyday life situations, such as when the child hates doing homework. In this case study, both the son and his father participated in separate sessions to resolve their individual triggers on the subject. They reported that the session resulted in a more relaxed child and a parent who responded to his current situation rather than his past experiences.

Case Study provided and written by: Myriam Nordemann
Certification: Practitioner and Instructor in Logosynthesis®
Role: Professional Counselor, Parental Coach
Website: www.myriam-nordemann.com
Location: Milan, Italy

Alex is a ten-year-old boy who had issues with doing his homework. He did not cooperate and was unwilling to complete the work. This created a lot of problems in class and tensions at home. His mother, Celia, was looking for help to resolve the issue.

The first online session was with Alex. Celia was also present. Alex started by telling me that he hates homework and doesn't want to do it. I asked him what goes on in his body when he has homework to do. He tells me that he feels "weird" things in his stomach. He gives it a SUDS rating of 7.

I prepared some pictures to show him. I asked him to tell me which one of the pictures represented the feeling in his stomach and the thoughts about doing his homework. He pointed to a picture of an angry face. We do a cycle for this image:

- *I retrieve all my energy bound up in the "image of this angry face" and take it to the right place in my Self.*
- Working pause.
- *I remove all non-me energy related the "image of this angry face" from all of my cells, all of my body and my personal space, and send it to where it truly belongs.*
- Working pause.
- *I retrieve all of my energy bound up in all of my reactions to the "image of this angry face" and take it to the right place in my Self.*

His stress dropped to 0 for this picture. He then felt stress about doing his homework. He rated this at a 4. I asked him to draw what the number represented and he drew an image of a child with a cloud above him.

We do another cycle of Logosynthesis on this image.

- *I retrieve all my energy bound up in this "image of the child with the cloud above him" and take it to the right place in my Self.*
- Working pause.
- *I remove all non-me energy related this "image of the child with the cloud above him" from all of my cells, all of my body and my personal space, and send it to where it truly belongs.*

- Working pause.
- I retrieve all of my energy bound up in all of my reactions to this "image of the child with the cloud above him" and take it to the right place in my Self.

After this cycle, he provided a SUDS rating of 0. As we explored what was happening, he expressed a belief that homework is useless and boring.

- I retrieve all my energy bound up in "the belief that homework is useless and boring" and take it to the right place in my Self.
- Working pause.
- I remove all non-me energy related to "the belief that homework is useless and boring" from all of my cells, all of my body and my personal space, and send it to where it truly belongs.
- Working pause.
- I retrieve all of my energy bound up in all of my reactions to "the belief that homework is useless and boring" and take it to the right place in my Self.

He now felt lighter and more serene and went out to play. I debriefed with Celia. I asked her whether she or her husband were concerned about this problem. She said that her husband, Kris, was the most concerned. I suspected that Alex's belief about homework had something to do with his father and that this could be resolved. I suggested that Kris also do a Logosynthesis session.

Between the two sessions, Celia told me that Alex had

changed a lot. He was much more cooperative when it came to organizing his homework and there was less tension about the subject.

Kris began his online session by telling me that, for him, homework was an obligation and represented a lack of freedom. He informed me that his son is like him in that he does not like authority. I listened further to his story. Kris reported that when he is forced to do something, he thinks of his father. He connected with specific thoughts, emotions, and physical sensations. The SUDS rating was 9. An image emerged of his father standing in front of him.

We labeled this as the trigger and applied a cycle of Logosynthesis:

- *I retrieve all my energy bound up in the "image of my father standing in front of me" and take it to the right place in my Self.*
- Working pause.
- *I remove all non-me energy related to the "image of my father standing in front of me" from all of my cells, all of my body and my personal space, and send it to where it truly belongs.*
- Working pause.
- *I retrieve all of my energy bound up in all of my reactions to the "image of my father standing in front of me" and take it to the right place in my Self.*

After the sentences, the SUDS was a 0. Kris no longer felt negatively about homework. However, he now worried that his son was doing as he had done and that he might spend sleepless nights doing his homework at the last minute. Another image emerged. He saw himself at the age of 13. It was four in the morning and he was in his room, working on a report about a squirrel.

We labeled this as the trigger and did another cycle of Logosynthesis:

- *I retrieve all my energy bound up in the "image of me working on the report at four in the morning" and take it to the right place in my Self.*
- *Working pause.*
- *I remove all non-me energy related to the "image of me working on the report at four in the morning" from all of my cells, all of my body and my personal space, and send it to where it truly belongs.*
- *Working pause.*
- *I retrieve all of my energy bound up in all of my reactions to the "image of me working on the report at four in the morning" and take it to the right place in my Self.*

After this cycle, the image was no longer stressful for Kris. He told me that suddenly he recognized that his son is different from him. He recognized that Alex has his own life. Kris told me that his son will not be like him and that he felt that he was going to build his life the way he wanted.

A few weeks later, Celia gave me some news.

She told me that Alex was much more relaxed: "If you

ask him to fetch something from the fridge, he does it willingly. Before, he would complain and grumble." She also told me that she felt he is less melancholic and appears liberated. Also, Kris told Celia that his way of looking at Alex had completely changed. Rather than seeing himself in his son, he sees Alex as the individual that he is!

In this situation, I worked with the family to resolve an issue that appeared related to the child. By working with both the son and the father, in two separate sessions, we were able to resolve distress related to doing homework.

Case Study 3: Resolving tension

Contributing to community organizations can play an important role in thriving in our times. We often find the work meaningful and rewarding. However, we may not feel comfortable when we are new to an established organization. We may work differently from other volunteers. Logosynthesis can be used to resolve feelings of tension and anxiety so that we can enjoy meaningful contribution.

Case Study provided and written by: Cathy Caswell
Certification: Practitioner and Instructor in Logosynthesis®
Role: Coach
Website: www.thehealthylivingplan.com
Location: Halifax, Canada

The 4-H Program has a 100-year history of contributing to rural communities, much of that contribution made possible by the support of incredible parent volunteers. Although many in the organization know the way things are done, the program is complicated to learn. For parents new to the organization, learning the program can feel intense. As they begin to take on volunteer roles, the tension often rises. The fun can be easily zapped when expectations are not clear or people are not pleased with the results.

I was speaking with Latisha, who is a parent volunteer. She expressed that she felt really frustrated when she attended regular meetings. She was at a loss as to what to do.

She didn't feel that she wanted to continue volunteering with this level of frustration. Others in the 4-H group had been involved for a long time and were quite specific about how things should be done. Latisha felt that she was being judged and she was struggling to learn how things were done. She believed that others should help her learn rather than be judgmental.

I asked her if she wanted to let go of the feeling. "Yes!" she replied.

When I asked her to notice the sensations she was experiencing, she readily reported tightness in her chest. She took some time to explore how distressing it felt when she walked into the meetings. She could sense the intensity. I asked her to rate the level of distress on a scale of 0-10, with 10 being the most distressing. She gave it a SUDS rating of 8.

I then asked Latisha to tell me what images, sounds, or other sensory perceptions she noticed. She noticed an image of the people in the room, sitting at the table in their usual seats. The image was clear and it was in front of her.

We labeled this image as the trigger to be used in a cycle of Logosynthesis:

- *I retrieve all my energy bound up in this "image of the people in the room" and take it to the right place in my Self.*
- Working pause.
- *I remove all non-me energy related to this "image of the people in the room" from all of my cells, all of my body and my*

- *personal space, and send it to where it truly belongs.*
- *Working pause.*
- *I retrieve all of my energy bound up in all of my reactions to this "image of the people in the room" and take it to the right place in my Self.*
- *Working pause.*

I asked her what she noticed. She felt better. The tension was gone and the people in the image were now smiling. She no longer felt the distress associated with the meetings.

I asked Latisha to rate the level of distress. She gave it a SUDS rating of 2. This felt like a good place to end the session.

Case Study 4: Setting boundaries

It is common to experience challenges in setting boundaries at work. When conditions suddenly change, it can be more difficult to set these boundaries while they have increased importance for our wellbeing. This example describes how Logosynthesis supports this work.

Case Study provided and written by: Heather Day
Certification: Master Practitioner and Trainer in Logosynthesis®
Role: Coach and Trainer
Website: www.heatherdaycoaching.com
Location: London, UK

A female manager, Jane, is part of a team working with the safety and well-being of children and young people. The job is often stressful, but Jane is a good manager and usually handles the high demands well. However, the recent lockdown measures due to Covid-19 meant enforced work-from-home practices. This compounded the level of stress that she experienced.

Jane came to the online coaching session presenting high levels of stress and anxiety. This was caused by her manager asking her to stand in for him in an important case review meeting, with only 10 minutes notice. Jane felt put on the spot, but equally found it hard to say no in the circumstances. Jane is a conscientious manager with a caring and responsible attitude. Having no time to prepare put her right on the edge of her comfort zone.

After agreeing to chair the meeting, Jane immediately experienced a strong sense of panic. She explained to me that in normal circumstances she would need at least an hour to prepare. I have worked with Jane for a while so she had previous experience using Logosynthesis. I asked her to connect back to the moment when she said yes to her boss. She immediately experienced a strong sensation of panic. She began to sweat and take shorter breaths. She had thoughts about what people would think of her. Jane had a perception of other people judging her. She had the thought that she was not doing her job properly. This was followed by the thought: "I'm not good at this." She sensed a feeling of helplessness. Her distress had a SUDS rating of 8.

When Jane was asked to explore the space around her in relation to this high level of anxiety, she immediately saw a dark tunnel in front of her. She felt like she was being sucked down into it. Now we had a clear image to work with. I had a feeling that what Jane was experiencing in the present related to more than one event. Her anxiety was being re-activated by the current trigger of being put on the spot. I used her words and offered her a cycle of Logosynthesis using the label "this perception of being sucked down a dark tunnel" and added "and all it represents."

- I retrieve all my energy bound up in this "perception of being sucked down a dark tunnel and all it represents" and take it to the right place in my Self.
- Working pause.
- I remove all non-me energy related to this "perception of being sucked down a dark tunnel and all it represents" from all of my cells, all of my body and my personal space, and send it to where it truly belongs.
- Working pause.
- I retrieve all of my energy bound up in all of my reactions to this "perception of being sucked down a dark tunnel and all it represents" and take it to the right place in my Self.
- Working pause.

Jane said the sentences aloud, allowing a short working pause in between, and drank water. Jane's SUDS rating had gone down to 4. She felt much calmer and her breathing returned to normal. The image of the tunnel had faded away to what she described as greyness.

I asked Jane: "What happens now, if your manager asks you to chair a meeting for him again at the last minute?"

Jane was now able to calmly state that she needed more notice to prepare. She no longer felt compelled to say yes in the same way, thereby taking on too much.

We had spoken about her manager in our previous coaching sessions. Jane felt that he was struggling and lacking in confidence. I highlighted the organizational dynamics at play. If a line manager or a leader is feeling out of their depth, they will try to pass on their responsibility for some tasks to others. The conscientious managers, like Jane, may end up to taking on more than their role dictates which leads to feeling overly responsible.

We had time left in our session. I had a sense there was more to explore because Jane's SUDS rating was still 4. As we continued to talk, she again used the words "not doing her job properly."

I asked: "On a scale of 1-100, how confident are you that you can do your job properly?"

She replied: "Ninety."

This was interesting. Jane felt confident within herself. Yet her anxiety rose when she thought about the perceptions of what others might think.

I asked: "Who or what is related to this perception that you are not doing your job properly?"

Immediately, Jane saw an image of her previous line manager, who was known as a bully. She recalled a time when he had used those exact words to her. She described the image of him as being angry and critical.

I offered Jane a second cycle of Logosynthesis, using the label of this "image of this critical, angry manager":

- *I retrieve all my energy bound up in this "image of this critical, angry manager" and take it to the right place in my Self.*
- Working pause.

- *I remove all non-me energy related to this "image of this critical, angry manager" from all of my cells, all of my body and my personal space, and send it to where it truly belongs.*
- *Working pause.*
- *I retrieve all of my energy bound up in all of my reactions to this "image of this critical, angry manager" and take it to the right place in my Self.*
- *Working pause.*

The cycle served to neutralize the frozen perception of her manager. Her SUDS rating went down to 0. Jane was back in the present and able to reflect on the meeting rationally. She realized that she had done a very good job, even at such short notice.

Logosynthesis is an empowering model to use in the workplace. Jane's feedback the next day was as follows: "I found the session very helpful. I feel much more relaxed and rejuvenated." I emailed Jane a week later to check in again. She was in a reflective and balanced place. "I'm stepping back from taking on too much," she said and added, "I'm taking the wider view that this is a job, and work is only a part of my life. It's just not worth getting stressed about."

Case Study 5: Focusing attention

When we aim to transition to new roles, we can experience behaviors that sabotage our efforts. We can get stuck in patterns that prevent us from taking the necessary steps to move forward. In this example, Logosynthesis is used to resolve the blocks that get in the way of required tasks and focus attention on what is important.

Case Study provided and written by: Shanda Woodin, MSW, RSW
Certification: Master Practitioner and Trainer in Logosynthesis®
Role: Counselor; Trauma specialist
Website: www.logosynthesis.ca/about
Location: Brighton, Canada

James is a serving military member. We have a strong therapeutic rapport from previous work. Since our last session, he has been deployed and returned from his tour overseas. Currently, he is enrolled in a course preparing for the next leadership rank.

James started the session by noticing that he appears to be "self-sabotaging with his assignments." He completes them, he said, yet not in his preferred manner or to his true ability. He works in a rushed state. James wondered if he has had ample opportunity to decompress from his deployment.

As a trauma specialist, I explored this aspect. There were no apparent or expressed trauma reactions from his tour. He expressed that he was "fighting something." He articulated thoughts of "I am not smart enough" and "I don't want to do it." These thoughts pertained both to the assignments and to advancing to the next rank. He also stated that he was opposing something. He expressed: "There is a part that…." I was eager to offer a cycle of Logosynthesis on "this opposing part" but our discussion evolved.

James continued describing the situation. He stated that the course assignments were insulting his intelligence, which did not seem to match his belief that "I am not smart enough." We had targeted this belief in past sessions. James wondered if he was going to accomplish his goal of continuing his education to achieve the next leadership rank.

I allowed James to continue. He then clearly stated a belief that he was "walking away from what he has worked so hard to get."

I provided James with a cycle of Logosynthesis, using this belief as the label:

- *I retrieve all my energy bound up in this "perception of walking away from what I have worked so hard to get" and take it to the right place in my Self.*
- *Working pause.*
- *I remove all non-me energy related to this "perception of walking away from what I have worked so hard to get" from all*

of my cells, all of my body and my personal space, and send it to where it truly belongs.

- Working pause.

- *I retrieve all of my energy bound up in all of my reactions to this "perception of walking away from what I have worked so hard to get" and take it to the right place in my Self.*

- Working pause.

I asked James to explore what he noticed. An image arose of "an open cage with him on the outside." He was perplexed and confused by this image because he did not have words to adequately express what this image represented. I explained that with Logosynthesis, we do not need to think about and understand what sensory images appear. I added the words "and everything it represents" to the label to capture what he did not understand. We labeled this trigger and applied another cycle of Logosynthesis:

- *I retrieve all my energy bound up in this "image of an open cage and everything it represents" and take it to the right place in my Self.*

- Working pause.

- *I remove all non-me energy related to this "image of an open cage and everything it represents" from all of my cells, all of my body and my personal space, and send it to where it truly belongs.*

- Working pause.

- I retrieve all of my energy bound up in all of my reactions to this "image of an open cage and everything it represents" and take it to the right place in my Self.
- Working pause.

James sighed and said it felt good. He expressed that he had wanted to share with me that, since doing past work, he has gained a sense of joy in things and he has been able to let go of angered responses. However, he has noticed that he has also been losing the ability to access or stay with "nice" emotions. Also, he expressed challenges in accessing the mental structure that he had previously used to successfully do his work. He explored the thought with curiosity, wondering why our past work was preventing him from doing his assignments.

I noted two pieces of information from his comments: the inability to stay focused on his course assignments and the inability to stay with joy-filled emotions. I asked for more information.

James was able to describe a time when he felt "overwhelming nice" but could not stay attuned to the emotion. I wondered if this was due to past experiences. We had worked on triggers related to "father" that limited his ability to obtain a university degree.

James smiled. He knew of many examples of experiencing this "overwhelming nice" feeling. He paused with a knowing look. He explained that he was hearing "many voices" with the same origin: his father. The voices were telling him "Don't do that." The voices were related to a time when he was overzealous or joyful as a young boy. I was familiar with this type of response. Parents tame their children as part of their parenting work to teach appropriate behavior. This can be experienced as a trigger. We labeled the trigger as "the words *don't do that.*" I guided James through a third cycle:

- I retrieve all my energy bound up in this "perception of the words Don't do that" *and take it to the right place in my Self.*
- Working pause.
- I remove all non-me energy related to this "perception of the words Don't do that" *from all of my cells, all of my body and my personal space, and send it to where it truly belongs.*
- Working pause.
- I retrieve all of my energy bound up in all of my reactions to this "perception of the words Don't do that" *and take it to the right place in my Self.*
- Working pause.

As the words worked their magic, James noticed a lovely memory surface. It was the memory of a mentor who had told him: "I've watched you grow."

We explored how he might respond when he had to complete course assignments in the future. He shared how he would write his assignment tonight so that he had time to let the course material simmer. He would review and rework the assignment in a few days. James said that this felt better than writing under the pressure of the due date. It seemed realistic that he could do this. Prior to our session, James noticed that he was procrastinating frequently yet knew the assignment was not too difficult for him. This feeling shifted even though we did not work directly on his stated inability to focus his attention on his assignments. This was a good place to end our one-hour session.

Case Study 6: Resolving a panic attack

Many people experience panic attacks in response to something that happens. Our normal coping strategies, such as deep breathing, may not offer sustained relief. We can resolve the distress by using the fast and easy method of Logosynthesis: connect with how we suffer; identify and locate the triggers; and restore the flow using the three specific sentences.

Case Study provided and written by: Mathias Egger
Certification: Practitioner and Instructor in Logosynthesis®
Role: Clinical psychologist
Website: www.mathias-egger.ch
Location: Ramosch, Switzerland

The starting point for my session with Mark related to panic attacks. The attacks occurred at night during the weeks that news about the Covid-19 pandemic escalated. Mark reported that his neck hurt. He experienced problems with swallowing and felt tightness. He didn't know about Logosynthesis but we'd known each other for a long time. I introduced the topic and he trusted me to guide him through the process.

Mark explained that in the last few weeks, panic attacks had built up at night. They were associated with thoracic pressure and tightness, heart palpitations, and strong anxiety. He had been watching his body closely. In fact, he had been obsessive about noticing any symptoms. Even with his often-praised breathing exercises, he had not been able to feel reassured. I indicated that this is not surprising because the exercises strengthen the focus on fear-based body perceptions. Mark told me that he recently had a medical examination and the test for Covid-19. The test result was negative.

Mark had been working on his own, using different strategies to deal with his panic attacks. He noticed that the fear had lessened overall but a few days prior to our meeting he had a migraine headache. His thoughts were circling less intensely but he wondered about psychosomatic or somatic causes. When I asked for clarification, he said that he often takes on the concerns of others.

I asked Mark who he cares about the most. He cares about his parents, especially for his mother, he said. He felt concerned and uncertain when he thinks about her. He rated the SUDS as 5 out of 10. I guided him to locate a sensory perception. He saw his mother in the room—on his left side—with all her fragility. We labeled this as the trigger and I guided him through a cycle of Logosynthesis:

- *I retrieve all my energy bound up in this "image of my mother with all her fragility" and take it to the right place in my Self.*
- Working pause.
- *I remove all non-me energy related to this "image of my mother with all her fragility" from all of my cells, all of my body and my personal space, and send it to where it truly belongs.*

- *Working pause.*
- *I retrieve all of my energy bound up in all of my reactions to this "image of my mother with all her fragility" and take it to the right place in my Self.*
- *Working pause.*

He felt a cozy warmth. He noticed a lightness, like cotton. I asked him what he noticed about the image of his mother. It had shifted. He now perceived that his mother was happy.

There was a slight residual tension remaining in his body. He felt this in his diaphragm region. He described "a pressure that feels like the outside of the palms of my hands pushing on my belly." We labeled this trigger as the "palms of the hand." I guided him through a second cycle of Logosynthesis:

- *I retrieve all my energy bound up in this "perception of the palms of the hand" and take it to the right place in my Self.*
- *Working pause.*
- *I remove all non-me energy related to this "perception of the palms of the hand" from all of my cells, all of my body and my personal space, and send it to where it truly belongs.*
- *Working pause.*
- *I retrieve all of my energy bound up in all of my reactions to this "perception of the palms of the hand" and take it to the right place in my Self.*
- *Working pause.*

Mark breathed deeply. He noticed that the pressure disappeared.

We returned to the first appearance of the panic attacks in his life. This triggered thoughts and sensations relating to loneliness and insecurity. As he connected with these feelings of distress, he perceived a "dark silence" around him. We labeled the trigger as the "dark silence." I guided Mark through another cycle of Logosynthesis:

- *I retrieve all my energy bound up in this "perception of dark silence" and take it to the right place in my Self.*
- Working pause.
- *I remove all non-me energy related to this "perception of dark silence" from all of my cells, all of my body and my personal space, and send it to where it truly belongs.*
- Working pause.
- *I retrieve all of my energy bound up in all of my reactions to this "perception of dark silence" and take it to the right place in my Self.*
- Working pause.

There seemed to be a lot of energy shifting during the processing of this cycle. Overall, he felt more strength in his back. The anxiety attacks seemed less threatening. He felt comfortable to leave the session here.

I received an email from Mark two weeks later, offering the following feedback:

"I am happy to send you a little update. I read the book

you gave me [*Letting It Go* by Laurie Weiss] with great interest after finding it in my inbox. As soon as I have felt insecurity or anxiety arise, I have formulated appropriate sentences. And it actually worked. I am amazed. I haven't had tightness in my chest since we talked, which of course I am very thankful for. Luckily, I haven't had a panic attack either. I am calm and taking time to rest, especially in the evening."

Case Study 7: Breathing through grief

Experiencing the loss of a loved one introduces a range of intense thoughts, emotions, and physical sensations, which can be difficult to describe to others. We do not want to let go of our loved ones. This example describes how Logosynthesis can be used to support individuals in the grieving process by gracefully restoring the flow of our energy to provide relief.

Case Study provided and written by: Cathy Caswell
Certification: Practitioner and Instructor in Logosynthesis®
Role: Coach
Website: www.thehealthylivingplan.com
Location: Halifax, Canada

I love the change in season from winter to spring. The days are longer, the sun is warmer and the colors are more vibrant. Yet not everyone is in a position to look forward to spring with anticipation. I spoke with a colleague recently who was struggling with moving forward since her mother passed away before Christmas, at the beginning of winter.

"I want to be on pause," she said. She was connecting with a sense of not wanting to go on to the next season without her mother. To me, this was understandable.

As she spoke about this transition, emotions started to surface. Anger. Regret. Sadness. To me, this also was understandable.

"I struggle to breathe. I went for a walk yesterday and my chest felt so heavy. I'm told to focus on my breathing and I try breathing techniques but it doesn't help," she said. I know from my work with Logosynthesis that these sensations can feel very intense, especially when connecting with grief and loss.

This is our starting point with Logosynthesis. How do you suffer? What are the thoughts, emotions, and sensations? We connect with the distress for a moment. Not to rationalize it or judge it but rather to acknowledge it.

I asked her to notice her level of distress on a scale of 0-10, with 10 being the most distressing. She rated it an 8.

I asked her to connect with this distress, gently guiding her and giving her time to notice what appears.

Is there an image, sound, or other sensory perceptions? Do not think about it. Simply notice.

"Ahhhh! I have an image."

"Can you locate the image?"

"Yes. It appears right in front of me."

From experience as a guide, when I sense that a client has located a distressing image that is very personal, I do not probe further. This can allow the client to stay better connected with the process. This can support deep healing because it helps to build trust and safety for the client.

We apply a cycle of Logosynthesis to "this image in front of me," allowing a pause for each sentence to process.

- *I retrieve all my energy bound up in this "image in front of me" and take it to the right place in my Self.*
- *Working pause.*
- *I remove all non-me energy related to this "image in front of me" from all of my cells, all of my body and my personal space, and send it to where it truly belongs.*
- *Working pause.*
- *I retrieve all of my energy bound up in all of my reactions to this "image in front of me" and take it to the right place in my Self.*
- *Working pause.*

"What do you notice now?" I asked.

"I can breathe."

"Can you imagine going for a walk without the heaviness?"

"Yes."

I checked in the next morning and asked how she was feeling.

"I slept really well last night. First time in months."

Of course, there will be many more distressing thoughts, emotions, and sensations that arise throughout the grief process. With an appropriate model like Logosynthesis, along with the support of an experienced guide for more difficult situations, hidden and frozen perceptions can be softened to help clients breathe again and move into the next season.

Case Study 8: Calming distress related to trauma

In our everyday lives, we can experience events that result in trauma. Others who do not experience the distress can have difficulty relating to our experience. This example demonstrates how Logosynthesis can be used by trained professionals to resolve the frozen perceptions to relieve the distress related to trauma.

Case Study provided and written by: Dr. Ineke Kersten
Certification: Master Practitioner and Trainer in Logosynthesis®
Role: Clinical Psychologist
Website: www.synthesepraktijk.nl
Location: Den Hague, The Netherlands

This case study is about Emily, who was suffering after being attacked during her evening walk. This walk is normally her precious moment of the day. It is meditative and offers her a moment for herself. The walk has now changed because she was in the wrong place at the wrong time. She was attacked from behind by an unknown man for no reason at all. She was knocked down and punched in the face. Her nose and left ankle were broken. She had severe abrasions in her face.

When I met with Emily, she was sitting across from me in a wheelchair. Her face was totally bruised, with a deep purple and yellow color. Her nose had been straightened in the emergency room. She told me about what happened.

She got emotional when she got to the moment of the attack.

I guide her to explore the images, sounds, and other sensory perceptions. In this case, she perceives more than one trigger. She labels them as "hearing the footsteps from behind" and "feeling the slaps on my face." I guide her with two cycles of Logosynthesis for these two significant moments.

- *I retrieve all my energy bound up in "the sound of hearing the footsteps from behind" and take it to the right place in my Self.*
- Working pause.
- *I remove all non-me energy related to the sound of "hearing the footsteps from behind" from all of my cells, all of my body and my personal space, and send it to where it truly belongs.*
- Working pause.
- *I retrieve all of my energy bound up in all of my reactions to the sound of "hearing the footsteps from behind" and take it to the right place in my Self.*
- Working pause.

After this first cycle, I offer the second cycle:

- *I retrieve all my energy bound up in "feeling of the slaps on my face" and take it to the right place in my Self.*
- Working pause.
- *I remove all non-me energy related to the "feeling of the slaps on my face" from all of my cells, all of my body and my personal space, and send it to where it truly belongs.*

- Working pause.
- *I retrieve all of my energy bound up in all of my reactions to the "feeling of the slaps on my face" and take it to the right place in my Self.*
- Working pause.

At the end of the processing, she said of her own accord that this moment is now in the past. The processing of the triggers using the Logosynthesis sentences brought her into the here and now. She left more calmly and with more confidence.

Ten days later, I spoke with Emily. She was still in the wheelchair. Her leg was horizontal and in a cast. She recently had an operation on her ankle. The bruises were fading. The wounds were recovering. There was still a thick, black scab on her lip.

Emily told me that she went back to the place where she was attacked. She was pleased that she was still able to experience the spot as a quiet, meditative place. She realized how much power she has in herself to be able to process this terrible experience.

Emily told me that she still suffers from a few images related to the attack. She labeled the triggers as "the image of this young man shooting into the reeds"; "this shadow" and "this darkness in me." I guided her through a cycle of Logosynthesis for each of these labels. With each cycle, she experienced a lot of emotions. I observed that there was a lot of energy shifting that was bound in these triggers.

To my surprise, at the end of the sentences, Emily was laughing. She had encountered the most distress with the image labeled "this darkness in me." As the energy shifted during this set of sentences, the black scab that was on her lip suddenly fell off. She felt that she was letting go of all the darkness. Laughing, she said, "What perfect timing!"

A few weeks later, we looked back at the situation. She was doing well, both physically and emotionally. She could look back at the event with a certain distance. She no longer re-experienced the event. She tried to give meaning to what happened to her. She stated: "If I can forgive the perpetrator, I can forgive myself more often if I don't function according to the high bar I set for myself." She also felt a great bond with her parents, who, she said, take such good and loving care of her. This is an example of how traumatic events can be treated well with Logosynthesis.

Author's note: This case study deals with a serious, traumatic event that was guided by an experienced clinical psychologist who is certified as a Master Practitioner in Logosynthesis®. It is provided to demonstrate how a guided intervention using Logosynthesis can change an individual's perception of an event. It is not meant to minimize the seriousness of the event.

Case Study 9: Eliminating a teacher's frustration

In our everyday lives, we can get stuck in patterns of reacting to others. Even though we feel frustrated by and guilty about how we respond, we may be unable to let go of the pattern. We can use Logosynthesis to resolve the triggers so that our responses to those around us create a more supportive environment.

Case Study provided and written by: Christin Aannerud
Certification: Master Practitioner and Trainer in Logosynthesis®
Role: Coach
Website: https://ich-du-wir.ch/
Location: Durnten, Switzerland

This case is about Ella, a teacher who booked a counseling session with me to resolve frustration at work. Every time she corrected essays by certain students, she became very frustrated. She felt that the students had not made sufficient effort. It became difficult to give fair and objective feedback. In addition, she knew that writing was not easy for these students and this made her feel guilty.

As Ella connected with the thoughts and emotions, I guided her to notice any images, sounds, or other sensory perceptions. She remembered a situation when she was 12 years old. She had written an essay. Her mother had told her that she could not hand in the essay because it was so bad.

We labeled this trigger and I offered a cycle of Logosynthesis:

- *I retrieve all my energy bound up in this "perception of my mother saying that the essay was so bad" and take it to the right place in my Self.*
- Working pause.
- *I remove all non-me energy related to this "perception of my mother saying that the essay was so bad" from all of my cells, all of my body and my personal space, and send it to where it truly belongs.*
- Working pause.
- *I retrieve all of my energy bound up in all of my reactions to this "perception of my mother saying that the essay was so bad" and take it to the right place in my Self.*
- Working pause.

At the end of the processing, Ella was in tears. She said that she was never good at writing essays; she always had bad grades. Again, I guided her to notice any images, sounds, or other sensory perceptions. She noticed the image of her language teacher. She stood on her left side. We labeled this trigger and applied a cycle of Logosynthesis:

- *I retrieve all my energy bound up in this "image of my language teacher on my left side" and take it to the right place in my Self.*
- Working pause.

- I remove all non-me energy related to this "image of my language teacher on my left side" from all of my cells, all of my body and my personal space, and send it to where it truly belongs.
- Working pause.
- I retrieve all of my energy bound up in all of my reactions to this "image of my language teacher on my left side" and take it to the right place in my Self.
- Working pause.

At the end of this cycle, Ella noticed an increased level of grief. She had the impression that the whole of society kept telling her that how she expressed herself was unclear, even bad. I asked her how she perceived this in society. She saw a field in the upper left corner where lots of people were arguing.

While it was not apparent to me how this related to marking essays, this was a frozen perception. We labeled this as the trigger and applied one more cycle of Logosynthesis:

- I retrieve all my energy bound up in this "image of the field with people arguing" and take it to the right place in my Self.
- Working pause.
- I remove all non-me energy related to this "image of the field with people arguing" from all of my cells, all of my body and my personal space, and send it to where it truly belongs.
- Working pause.

- *I retrieve all of my energy bound up in all of my reactions to this "image of the field with people arguing" and take it to the right place in my Self.*
- *Working pause.*

At the end of processing this cycle, Ella looked up and smiled. In a follow-up conversation, Ella noted that she was able to correct all the essays from all of her students without frustration. She even arranged conversations with the students who had difficulty writing essays and was able to encourage and support her students. Ella noted that some of her students had even felt comfortable enough to take pleasure in writing: "I don't know where to start."

Case Study 10: Building a student's confidence

School years are an important time for growth and development. In addition to formal learning, we form relationships and learn how to interact with others. At times, we may struggle to feel confident and to fit in with friends. When we learn to let go of what stands in the way of our confidence, we are able to thrive.

Case Study provided and written by: Myriam Nordemann
Certification: Practitioner and Instructor in Logosynthesis®
Role: Professional counselor, parental coach
Website: www.myriam-nordemann.com
Location: Milan, Italy

This case study is about Clara, a 12-year-old who is struggling to feel confident about her upcoming exams. At our first meeting, she explored her level of confidence to pass the exam. We explored the thoughts, emotions, and body sensations associated with passing the exam. She rated her stress level as 10 out of 10. She rated her confidence at 9 out of 100.

She explored what appeared in the form of images, sounds, or other sensory perceptions. An image emerged of a past school episode where other students teased her.

- *I retrieve all my energy bound up in this "image of students teasing me" and take it to the right place in my Self.*

- Working pause.

- *I remove all non-me energy related to this "image of students teasing me" from all of my cells, all of my body and my personal space, and send it to where it truly belongs.*
- *Working pause.*
- *I retrieve all of my energy bound up in all of my reactions to this "image of students teasing me" and take it to the right place in my Self.*
- *Working pause.*

At the completion of this cycle, Clara rated her stress level again. The SUDS had moved from 10 to 4. She rated her level of confidence as 80. She was comfortable to end the meeting with a lower SUDS rating and higher degree of confidence.

During our second meeting, Clara explored her thoughts, emotions, and body sensations using drawings. She created drawings that represent thoughts, memories, and people related to the issue of lack of confidence for the exam. She talked about her distress related to a friend who had made a comment in the past. She identified the image. We labeled this trigger and applied a cycle of Logosynthesis:

- *I retrieve all my energy bound up in this "image of my friend making a comment" and take it to the right place in my Self.*
- *Working pause.*
- *I remove all non-me energy related to this "image of my friend*

> making a comment" from all of my cells, all of my body and my personal space, and send it to where it truly belongs.

- Working pause.
- I retrieve all of my energy bound up in all of my reactions to this "image of my friend making a comment" and take it to the right place in my Self.
- Working pause.

At the end of this cycle, she rated her level of distress as 0 out of 10. She rates her level of confidence as 90 out of 100. She felt this was a good place to end the session.

Her third appointment was on the eve of her exams. She told me that, from our first session, she was able to let go of the fear of judgment. From our second session, she was able to let go of the feeling of being less than the others.

She now rated her confidence as 90 out of 100. I asked her why she didn't rate it at 100. She told me that she didn't want to give her best because she didn't want to be noticed. If she did give her best, others would have something to say about it. She was worried about the way other people look at her. I guided Clara through a simple, advanced Logosynthesis technique to build confidence. Clara then rated her confidence at 100 out of 100. She said she would go to the exam with her head held high.

I then summarized the work that we did together and helped her integrate the changes that were taking place. I asked her to make a drawing that represented her mood and experience. She drew a picture of a tree with a shining star at the top. She was the star, Clara said. There were a lot of stars on the tree representing the other people. There were also some black stars because she had "erased" those from her life.

Clara wrote: "To be happy, you have to love each other and love everyone with their good and bad. We have to be with the people who love us and accept us for who we are and we must never change to please others".

Case Study 11:
Self-coaching during times of transition

Retirement is a remarkable time as we transition from a working career that often defines much of our identity. It can be especially exceptional when our world suddenly changes at the same time as we plan to transition to a new phase in our life. Logosynthesis provides a simple and powerful model to find comfort in moving forward.

Case Study provided and written by: Julie Jacinthe Arsenault, MSW, RSW
Certification: Master Practitioner in Logosynthesis®
Role: Psychotherapist
Location: New Richmond, Quebec, Canada

The pandemic situation which emerged in the world in early 2020 marked the beginning of an exceptional and challenging time. This was especially true for those of us who had not experienced such a loss of freedom and uncertainty in our lifetime. Like most people, I experienced a wide range of emotions. In my professional life, I anticipated that the spring of 2020 would be a time of transition to retirement. I prepared for and anticipated lots of time to enjoy a new, stress-free lifestyle. I dreamed of attending to my artistic passions, including gardening, photography, and singing. I also planned to travel with my husband. Suddenly, these plans were no longer possible.

I knew that it was important to adapt to the changes in my life. I felt that I was struggling with my feelings. As a mental health psychotherapist with a specialty in trauma work, I realized how much of my social activities helped to maintain a healthy balance with my professional life. I knew about the impact of social isolation. I knew that self-coaching with Logosynthesis could support this transition to help me feel better.

During the spring of 2020, I experienced changes with my connection to my family, my workplace, and my community. I lost physical connection with my immediate family. I felt the impact of the immediate cessation of family gatherings and celebrating important family events.

I experienced the loss of connection with my workplace. I was no longer able to see my clients in person.

I also experienced the loss of connection with my community. My French-Canadian culture is strongly anchored in social connection and I felt a strong need to connect. I felt the impact of stopping all of my cultural and recreational activities. This included participation in a choir of a hundred singers preparing for a big concert, the local book club, weekly yoga classes, and the local cinema club.

I was also aware of the impact of Covid-19 on the world around me. I felt compassion for the underprivileged, health care workers, and front-line workers. I also felt compassion for the victims of Covid-19 and for people grieving their loved ones without proper grieving rituals. I felt the need to help and to contribute.

I explored these many impacts of Covid-19 in my personal and professional life. I decided to use Logosynthesis to resolve what bothered me as issues arose. I started by connecting with my thoughts, emotions, and physical sensations in the moment:

- *My thoughts were anchored in the belief that I needed to adapt to the situation. I didn't like the disorganization of my work schedule. I knew that I did not want to fall into the path of anxiety.*
- *My emotions included disbelief, fear, anxiety, uncertainty, sadness, irritability, agitation, and frustration.*
- *My sensations centered around an edginess. I felt that had to keep busy, which I compared to a feeling of being hyperactive.*

Each time, as I connected with what was bothering me in the moment, I rated the distress. I identified and located the images, sounds, and other sensory perceptions. I labeled the trigger (X) and applied a cycle of Logosynthesis:

- *I retrieve all my energy bound up in this perception of "X" and take it to the right place in my Self.*
- *Working pause.*
- *I remove all non-me energy related to this perception of "X" from all of my cells, all of my body and my personal space, and send it to where it truly belongs.*

- 🌀 Working pause.
- 🌀 *I retrieve all of my energy bound up in all of my reactions to this perception of "X" and take it to the right place in my Self.*
- 🌀 Working pause.

I used Logosynthesis to guide my self-coaching on these many thoughts, emotions, and sensations between mid-March and June 2020. I experienced the following outcomes:

- *I felt calmer and more focused.*
- *I rediscovered that flexibility is key.*
- *I felt more open to possibilities within my work schedule, including a way of working from home using Zoom.*
- *I contributed to my workplace website enhancement.*
- *I felt a deepening connection with nature, including plants, insects, birds, and animals.*
- *I felt more engaged in various forms of contemplation.*
- *I reconnected with my creative self.*
- *I enjoyed time writing in my journal and composing haikus.*

I have discovered that using Logosynthesis to support self-coaching has helped me find a purpose during this period of transition. I now feel able to adjust my initial plan to retire. I will adopt a mid-term plan and postpone my retirement. I will create time to rest and take more time off. As a result of my self-coaching with Logosynthesis, I also feel deep gratitude for all the privileges in my life.

Case Study 12:
Letting go of the need to fight so hard

We may be familiar with thoughts, emotions, or physical sensations that are simply part of who we are. We have always known the pattern and we have learned to live with it. In times of change, the pressure can build and the patterns no longer work. Logosynthesis offers a guided method to resolve the energy field to support our health and productivity.

Case Study provided and written by: Cathy Caswell
Certification: Practitioner and Instructor in Logosynthesis®
Role: Coach
Website: www.thehealthylivingplan.com
Location: Halifax, Canada

I have included this case study to show how the energy field created by our parents' experiences can influence our reactions. It also demonstrates how to use Logosynthesis to resolve these patterns. Without first-hand experience of the shifts that can occur with Logosynthesis, I can appreciate that this story may be difficult to comprehend. I encourage you to be curious and open to possibility. For those who do have training in Logosynthesis or experience with other forms of energy work, you may recognize a similar personal experience.

In June 2018, I attended my first Logosynthesis Summer Academy in Germany. This is an annual, five-day seminar to learn new theory and to work on our own personal development. I didn't really know what to expect so I decided that I would just go with the flow. I was aware that the work to resolve what bothers me involves working in layers and that I often encountered themes that related to hard work and being heard.

As I approached my work for the week, I knew what I wanted to work on. In my everyday life, I was surrounded by a wonderful group of brilliant, respectful men who nonetheless caused me frustration because I felt they didn't listen to me. *They should listen to me!* I recognized that I spoke louder and more forcefully when I needed them to take notice. I was often considered one of the guys, which worked well until I came to them with an idea that was new or different. I came to appreciate that their intent was sincere but their response was to shut down an alternative viewpoint when it didn't fit their framework. So, when I felt shut down, I spoke more aggressively or I left in a huff. I recognized that this energy wasn't overly helpful in getting anyone to listen and yet, in the moment, that was my reaction and I felt justified in responding in this manner.

My goal through the seminar was to resolve the issue. I knew that these respectful men should listen to me and I was not prepared to let go of this belief. It made sense to me and it was important. I believed I needed this intensity to fight for what was important. I approached the issue with curiosity and intrigue. I already had a sense from earlier work with Willem that this energy was stuck in the field of my mother. I was guided through a session to further resolve what was bothering me. As I explored, I had a sense that this field of "smart, dominant men who wouldn't listen to me" was big. It was more than any one person. It felt like an impenetrable force. I was able to locate a perception of this force in front of me. I was guided to apply a Logosynthesis cycle.

- *I retrieve all my energy bound up in the "perception of this force in front of me" and take it to the right place in my Self.*
- *Working pause.*
- *I remove all non-me energy related to the "perception of this force in front of me" from all of my cells, all of my body and my personal space, and send it to where it truly belongs.*
- *Working pause.*
- *I retrieve all of my energy bound up in all of my reactions to the "perception of this force in front of me" and take it to the right place in my Self.*
- *Working pause.*

At the end of the processing, I was asked to note what was happening. I calmly stated: "I will not listen." Astrid, our supervisor for the session, noted the shift from "They should listen" to "I will not listen."

The next day, I could tell there was something that was still bothering me around these words. I was firm and agitated in my statement: "I will not listen." Astrid offered to guide me to explore further. We had learned about energetic fields as part of the theory in the seminar. The field of a parent can have a strong influence in shaping our beliefs and experiences. Using an advanced mapping process, I could easily connect with my mother's frustration. She had fallen in love and wanted to emigrate to Canada. Her commanding father was very adamant that this was not possible. She was the youngest in a very large family. Everyone meant well but no one supported her wish.

I connected with the feelings of my mother. The feeling of having fallen in love with a smart young man who was going to Canada, of her entire family telling her she could not go, and of her saying "I will not listen!" It felt very intense!

Astrid guided me through a modified version of the Logosynthesis sentences. As the words processed, I noticed a distinct shift. I do not have to fight so hard!

To this day, I don't feel that I have to fight so hard. And when I don't fight so hard, others are better able to listen. I am now able to recognize how this energy has impacted my work experiences over the years and I am better able to recognize patterned behavior in others. I continue to notice my responses around this theme and process the layers. I take things at my pace, knowing that I have a model to resolve my reactions when I am ready.

CHAPTER 5

Integrating Logosynthesis into everyday living

*When we, as individuals,
shift how we respond in our groups,
the dynamics change.
When we collectively learn to shift how we react,
our impact is amplified.*

Thriving in my everyday life

In the first four chapters of this book, I described how we can react when our lives change in an instant and identified how we can navigate this change as individuals in our families, our workplaces, and our communities. I've presented Logosynthesis to help move beyond our stuck patterns of behavior to take meaningful action. I've also offered case studies to demonstrate how this one fast and easy method can be used to calm reactions for a wide variety of issues. In this chapter, I will describe how I have integrated Logosynthesis into my everyday living and how this can help you clear your path in this changing world.

The Healthy Living Plan has been created to help you recognize and shift your reactions to clear your path forward, for yourself and in support of others. You can connect with The Healthy Living Plan through my website and through social media. You can also connect with me directly through my author website and social media. Contact details are available in the Appendix.

The work of The Healthy Living Plan rests on five pillars.

I will describe the importance of each pillar and how they work together to create flow in our lives. I will then offer a simple guide to allow you to start using your reactions to resolve what gets in the way of your purpose, before you take action. You will begin to notice a sense of connection, ease and flow that I associate with extraordinary living.

Throughout my university studies, my corporate career, and my many volunteer activities, healthy living has been a strong interest. I registered The Healthy Living Plan website in 2013 to design a health management program for the pharmacy I owned with my husband David. We planned to combine our expertise in pharmacy and dietetics to support individuals in making healthy lifestyle changes. I realized from my experience in both dietetics and marketing that we often know what we should do to support a healthy lifestyle but we struggle with taking appropriate action. Our patterns of behavior get in the way of healthy lifestyle choices. When I met Willem later that year, I was intrigued with his work because I recognized that Logosynthesis offered a unique solution to support these lifestyle changes.

As I began to use Logosynthesis in my everyday life, I began to feel calmer and more focused. As I shifted my reactions, those around me shifted their responses. I realized that Logosynthesis could not only help me, it could help others feel better. I knew that stress and anxiety had a negative health impact on many people. I was eager to share what I learned. I engaged in passionate conversations with my family, local politicians, business leaders, and community volunteers to explain how Logosynthesis could support healthy living. I was stuck in the belief that others needed to know this information because it was important for their health. I was committed to help them understand the work. I felt intensity in this belief because I sensed that people around me were struggling and that their lives didn't need to be so difficult. I believed that all they needed was the information and they could use it to make their life better.

You can probably predict where this story is going. My friends, families, and colleagues didn't understand the work or the intensity of my interest. They didn't understand how this new model worked. They had their own preferred coping techniques. They felt more comfortable with generally accepted methods. I knew to step down but I felt a drive to share the information to create awareness.

The Logosynthesis community provided great support through in-person seminars and an online Facebook group. I was reminded that people needed to be ready for this new information in order to embrace it. But how could I tell if they were ready?

In early 2016, I asked a question in our Facebook group to help me better understand. Julie, a respected colleague, suggested that I could explore my reactions to waiting. If I was bothered by waiting, it was my opportunity to resolve my trigger so that I was no longer bothered! I could use Logosynthesis to calm my reactions related to "waiting until people are ready for this information" so that I would be better able to take meaningful action.

I received Julie's response on a Saturday evening while enjoying a glass of wine. I had an immediate reaction to her suggestion. "But people are suffering and they don't need to suffer so much!" I thought. "Logosynthesis is so easy and people simply don't know about it!"

Although I had this immediate reaction, I respected Julie's advice so I took the time to follow her suggestion:

- I connected with my thoughts: I had worked so hard in so many aspects of my life and I now realized that these situations didn't have to feel so difficult. I had observed how people around me were struggling in everyday life; I felt sure that Logosynthesis could help them feel better; I knew that the work was so simple yet no one knew about it; I thought about what cues I would use to know when people were ready to learn about the work.
- I connected with my emotions: I felt agitated, frustrated, and angry. "They should know about this!" I thought. "They don't have to suffer so much!"
- I connected with my physical sensations: I could feel tightness in my throat; my jaw was clenched and my brow was furrowed.
- I rated the SUDS at 7 out of 10.

I then recognized this response from an earlier point in my life. I was diagnosed with Celiac Disease at the age of 21. I had suffered my entire childhood from undiagnosed

Celiac Disease. Even though I experienced a number of classic symptoms and many obscure symptoms, the doctor had told me and my parents that there was nothing wrong with me. At that time, there was no internet and most medical books contained one short paragraph on the topic. I had suffered for years when all I needed to do was avoid gluten to feel better. The doctor simply was not aware of the solution.

"They should know about this!"

My doctor's office came to mind, with my doctor telling my mother: "Don't bother bringing her back, there is nothing wrong with her." I recognized that this trigger activated a strong, frozen reaction. I believed the doctor should have known about Celiac Disease. He should not have dismissed me and my mother.

I used this frozen perception to apply a cycle of Logosynthesis. As I allowed the words to do their work, I felt much calmer. I was able to acknowledge that we did not know about Celiac Disease at the time but we learned. I acknowledged that I am now healthy. When I was diagnosed, I played a role in advocacy, awareness, and education at a local and national level.

I revisited my initial concern about waiting until people were ready to learn about Logosynthesis. I understood that my agitation was related to seeing people suffer when a simple solution was available—but people did not know about it. I felt calmer. I knew that people would learn. I could play a role in advocacy, awareness, and education. I felt more patience and compassion to help others learn.

I continued to share information about Logosynthesis and I continued to value the feedback from others. My daughters called me out when they felt that I was pushing my beliefs on other people. This was not my intent but they noticed my reactive behavior. I wanted to help others and my daughters helped me to realize that I had my own work to do first.

During the Covid-19 pandemic, I felt fine but I was aware that many people were struggling. Once again, I knew that Logosynthesis could help them feel better. I believed that they should know about the work but they either didn't have the information or didn't understand how to use it.

My earlier work to resolve triggers on this issue benefited me when we were faced with the pandemic. I didn't experience these triggers so I didn't have to do the work again. I was better able to remain calm and focused. I let people know that I was available. I posted a YouTube video to allow people to freely access the method on their own time, when they were ready. I shared information on my website and through social media posts. I was able to coach online. I continued my training and obtained certification as an Instructor in Logosynthesis®. I focused on writing the manuscript for this book. I was able to create resources to help others benefit from Logosynthesis. Rather than feeling stressed that others should know about this work, I was able to focus on actions to make the information accessible to those who were interested. I shared stories to help others understand. I engaged with the Logosynthesis community to learn about their experiences. And sure, I still reacted at times but I have compassion for where I am in my journey. I don't feel that I have to be perfect.

You will recognize that, through this process, I did not focus on changing others. I simply focused on changing my reactions to others. To me, this is the power of healthy living. My experience with Logosynthesis has helped me to recognize that I benefit when I look after myself first. When I am aware of my reactions, I can shift my response to create an environment that feels more supportive for others. I am then in a position to take action towards my goals, rather than getting stuck in the drama. I focus on using this one simple and powerful model to feel better, as an individual who contributes to my family, my workplace, and my community.

Supporting you to thrive in everyday life

The Healthy Living Plan rests on five pillars. Each pillar addresses a specific element of what it means to thrive. This holistic approach to health embraces the power of our Essence and our human nature. This section will highlight each pillar and offer a guide to support you to clear your own path for extraordinary living. The pillars are as follows:

THE HEATHY LIVING PLAN

attention to self care

a supportive environment

progress towards goals with one simple and powerful model for individuals in groups

Pillar 1: Attention to self-care

You may be familiar with the feeling that self-care sometimes feels like a chore. We receive lots of messages from the media and other people telling us what we need to do to stay healthy: eat the right foods; achieve the proper weight; exercise regularly; get the right amount of sleep; make time for relaxation; and the list goes on. When we consider these directives along with work and family priorities, it can feel stressful.

Based on my training in Logosynthesis, I now define self-care as "paying attention to my reactions and resolving my triggers to feel better." I am now better able to enjoy every day routines that are naturally healthier. I feel more relaxed so I do not feel the need for a rigid plan to make healthy choices.

We have been conditioned to be strong and to power through our challenges. In many cases, the more challenging the situation, the more energized we feel because our "fight" mode is activated. While this can feel resourceful in getting us through a crisis, this is a reactive mode. And this response can trigger reactions in those around us. When we are in this mode, we feel closed and defensive. This does not allow the flow of energy that supports us to thrive on a sustained basis through change and uncertainty.

As we tune in to our energy in these situations, we can use our reactions as information to calm our response. This may feel a little strange in the beginning but it allows us to access an open, creative mode. This proved to be very beneficial for me when Kraft Foods was purchased by Heinz in 2015. There was an increased focus on efficiency but Kraft was already a highly efficient company. One of the carrots provided for hard work was bonus pay for achieving results. If we all worked harder, we would be rewarded. Before my introduction to Logosynthesis, I would embrace this call to action but I could now see more clearly how we were all reacting to the push to work harder. I recall a conversation with one of our vice presidents in sales around the concept of working hard. My comment was that we would benefit if people worked a little less hard. I received a surprised and questioning look. I explained that when everyone was so focused on working hard, this busyness did not allow space to think about how we could best deliver our results. Everyone was so busy doing things that it created more work for other people and we lost focus on the customer. We started to make more mistakes. When we felt overwhelmed with the workload, our reactions resulted in unproductive conversations which took away from meaningful action.

It was easy to get frustrated with coworkers who did not understand my workload and held unrealistic expectations. I used the Empty Chair exercise, as described in Chapter 3, to help me improve relationships with my coworkers. This simple exercise shifted my frozen reactions, allowing for better conversations to work together. My self-work with Logosynthesis supported me to achieve what I was being asked to do.

During this time, I could find lots of people who validated that I was doing a great job and I was not the one who had to change. When I know I am right, I tend to fight harder to change the other person or the situation. When the stakes are high, I tend to fight even harder. In my workplace, this was hailed as a positive trait: passion.

But as I shifted my focus to simply resolving my triggers to calm my reactions, I was better able to present my ideas. When I owned my role in this dance of interactions, I was better able to lead the way for others. This is self-care. It supports us in being gentle with ourselves and with others, even when conditions are demanding. There is frozen energy bound in our beliefs, our life experiences, authoritative voices, and our cultural influences that convince us that we are right. We feel in control of our situation but we also get triggered when conditions change or don't meet our expectations.

I have noticed that I can be very attached to my beliefs. To support my ongoing self-care, I've found it helpful to take the perspective of challenging my "interesting" beliefs. If the behavior of others bothers me, Willem reminds me is always my work to do. I am quite certain that if anyone other than Willem told me this, I would have argued and walked away. Obviously, he did not know my situation or he would recognize that I was right. I could find lots of people to agree with me. I have come to appreciate that Willem reminds me of my uncles. I recall their mentoring.

"Always challenge your interesting beliefs Cathy."

I am human. I resisted doing my own work. But I was curious and I challenged my "interesting beliefs". I trusted the process. I let go of energy stuck in the belief that others had to change. I felt better.

When I view beliefs from a position of curiosity, as directed by Willem and my uncles, I find it much easier to see alternatives. For example, I hold strong beliefs that everyone should work hard and that we should all help each other. These are not bad beliefs to hold in our society. But I have come to appreciate that based on my upbringing, I have considerably more energy bound in these beliefs than most of my peers and this intensity gets expressed in my everyday habits and routines. I feel frustrated when others don't work hard or don't do their share of the work. I feel guilty when I don't work hard. How I react influences how others feel around me. When conditions become more demanding, this energy can become dysfunctional. When I am curious to resolve my triggers, my energy shifts so that I feel more relaxed with my work and others are not triggered by my intensity. This creates space to actually get the job done.

This self-care work is not about being right or wrong. This is about getting unstuck from the thoughts, emotions, and physical sensations that trigger my reactive behavior. When I learn to let go of my need to control, I feel better, and those around me are able to feel better too. And when we feel better, we are better able to appreciate our differences and focus on what is important to each of us.

Self-care requires a willingness to focus internally rather than externally. As humans, we often react automatically to the world around us. That is how we survive. As humans, we also have an ability to thrive by connecting with our world at a higher level of consciousness. When we are not comfortable or we feel threatened, we respond in survival mode. When we feel comfortable and safe, we are better able to thrive and to express creativity.

Willem continues to reinforce the importance of self-care. For every problem I present, he reminds me that if it bothers me, it is my work to do. I have come to appreciate the tremendous power in this realization. If my coworker does something that is not fair and it bothers me, I have the power to shift how I respond. From this position, I am no longer triggered by distressing thoughts, emotions and sensations. I am no longer stuck in patterns of reacting. I can *act*. That is self-care.

Pillar 2: A supportive environment

A supportive environment is a space that feels safe for everyone in the group. Each of us has our own sense of what feels safe and supportive, based on our culture and our previous experiences. We each contribute to the dynamics of a group and we each have a role in creating a supportive environment through attention to self-care. We each contribute to a supportive environment by resolving our own issues first. In other words, we create a supportive environment for others by attending to our own triggers and reactions. We begin by becoming aware of how we automatically respond when our frozen perceptions trigger frozen reactions. If we want our children to feel safe, we benefit from resolving what bothers us so that we feel safe and calm. If we want our employees to feel productive at work, we benefit from resolving our triggers in response to the demands and uncertainty of our own situation. If we want others to be calm, we benefit from recognizing how we activate others so that we can calm our response.

A supportive environment plays a key role in helping us thrive. We contribute to a supportive environment by doing our own work first. But when we do not feel comfortable or safe, it can be very challenging to do our own work. We may need a trusting relationship with a coach, counselor or therapist to help us with this work. Our automatic response is to react in patterned ways. We deny that we need help or we avoid the issue. When we allow ourselves to be vulnerable and trust the process, we can resolve what bothers us and we all benefit.

It's worth noting that what feels safe or supportive for one individual may not feel safe for another. When someone feels safe, they may easily assume that others feel safe. In diverse groups, it can be challenging to recognize what feels right for each person. This is the challenge of culture. One person can require a very high degree of support in order to perform. One person can also greatly reduce the perceived comfort of the group, based on how they react to others. If we are familiar with the group, we may feel comfortable despite high levels of reactive behavior. If we are new to the group, we may feel uncomfortable despite the group behaving according to their norms. Each individual in the group contributes to the level of safety and support felt in the total group. Individuals in positions of authority in the group have greater power to influence the group dynamics, either positively or negatively.

When there is increased levels of change and

uncertainty, individuals are more likely to get triggered and display reactive behavior in the group. The group therefore offers a lower level of support for all members. A new person may feel insecure and require an even higher level of support. Individuals will change to fit in with the group. The group will change based on the influence of the individual. Relationships develop over time.

I recognize the importance of creating a supportive environment for people to learn about Logosynthesis. As I described at the beginning of this chapter, when I first learned about Logosynthesis, I felt that everyone needed to know this information and I was eager to share it. People did not understand how three sentences could resolve what bothered them, so I was quick to explain and to demonstrate. The conversations were often in social settings and it did not always feel comfortable for people to talk about what bothered them in this space. We required a more supportive environment to learn. Although I recognize the value of curiosity in feeling safe to explore something new, I also recognize that my response to others is important in creating feelings of support, understanding, and compassion.

Through this work, I now have a deeper appreciation for the value of creating safety through supportive environments. In the past, if someone was argumentative, I would engage. If someone felt anxious, I would offer advice. If someone was emotional, I would be scared that I might make things worse. I am now more aware of how I respond and I do my own work first. Over time, I am better able to remain calm and listen. I am better able to simply be present for the other person. This is what I mean by a supportive environment.

I recognize that when I get triggered, my reaction can feel uncomfortable for others. The tone of my voice. The shift in my posture. The look on my face. These automatic responses, or frozen reactions, trigger a defensive reaction in others. If you sense that I am anxious because you are anxious, you will probably close in rather than open up. You may change the subject, feel uncomfortable, or walk away. When you are scared how I might respond when you are not feeling well, you may want to be alone. In a supportive environment, we can allow each other to simply be.

To support those around us, there is value in "holding space." At times, the structure of the Logosynthesis method provides sufficient support to allow me to connect with what bothers me so I can self-coach and simply let it go. For intense feelings, I need the support of a guide. The guide uses the same method that is used for self-coaching, with the added benefit that I am able to follow the process without backing out when it feels uncomfortable.

I know many people who would love to relieve distress in their lives. I also know many people who are looking to support others to relieve distress. People who are suffering are often open to trying something new to experience relief. They look to other people for validation. They are perceptive to words, facial expressions, posture, and tone of voice. I now recognize the importance of being supportive, without judgement. I know many people who would benefit from Logosynthesis and are interested to try the method. I have seen how the reactions of those around them and of professionals with other fields of training trigger their reactions, making them hesitant to try Logosynthesis. The learning will come with time, as each of us does our own work first to feel greater levels of compassion.

At times, this can be challenging. Compassion involves a conscious awareness of what the other person is experiencing. If we spend our entire life being treated like royalty, we cannot feel what it is like to be abandoned. If we have been the star of everything we ever attempted, we cannot feel what it is like to be constantly knocked down. If we have been surrounded by loving adults, we cannot feel what it is like to be abused. It can be difficult to be compassionate when we can't relate to the feeling. When I do my own work first and with a guide, I realize what it feels like to be vulnerable so I can have more compassion for what others experience.

Pillar 3: Progress towards goals

A key element of thriving involves progress towards goals. We learn to thrive when our life has meaning and we are connected to purpose. Our goals do not need to be grandiose, elaborate, or complicated. We thrive when we connect with what inspires our heart.

We are individuals and we live in a world that is organized in groups. Our families, workplaces, and communities are held together by collective attitudes and cultural beliefs. In many of our societies, we place significant value on individual achievement. We work hard. We strive for wealth. We accumulate resources. As we gain resources, we may gain control of our groups. We begin to associate success with our position within our groups.

We often define our goals to focus on external measures, such as the accumulation of friends, wealth, and possessions. External factors certainly have a significant influence on our ability to control our external conditions. If we have money, we have resources to change our situation. If we don't like our house, we can buy a new house. If we don't like our partner, we can afford to venture forward on our own. If we don't like our job, we can quit. In normal conditions, we may feel comfortable with this level of goal-setting. We may not pause to reassess our goals because our life is comfortable.

When our world suddenly changes, we may experience unexpected loss. Things we have worked hard to achieve may be suddenly gone. We experience factors that are beyond our control and our measures of progress may highlight a disconnect between effort and results. It is easy to get distracted by our attitudes and beliefs, both our own and the influence of others. We get stuck in questioning whether decisions are fair, others are doing their share, and the level of compensation for our efforts. Learning to resolve what bothers us allows us to move beyond these reactive patterns to take meaningful action.

Listening to our inner voice allows us to shift our goal-setting to better connect with what gives our life meaning. Logosynthesis supports us in learning to guide this process to follow our heart rather than getting stuck in our head. When we connect with what is really important, we are better able to identify what stands in the way and resolve what bothers us. I now recognize that many of the blocks that I have experienced in my life are energetic blocks. Energetic blocks, in the form of attitudes and beliefs, can be resolved using Logosynthesis. As we free our energy to connect with what gives our life meaning, we are better able to embrace the challenges we face.

For example, I have identified that helping others is meaningful to me. It has always been important to me to volunteer in my community, such as the Canadian Celiac Association, the Parent Teacher Committee at my daughters' school, and with their sports teams. I enjoyed this involvement but there was a limit on what I could offer. One of the triggers that I resolved related to my mother's encouragement to volunteer. She said she would have liked to volunteer more but she was always too busy. This was understandable given that she raised eight children on a busy farm, and with no extended family nearby. In relation to her experience, I had a much easier life. I felt that I was in a much better position to do more. When I resolved this trigger, I was better able to choose what I wanted to do rather than feel that I should do it all. The "should" was gone.

We live in this world with others and they will have an influence on what we create. There is beauty and power when we work together towards collective goals. This does not mean that we need to lose focus on our unique purpose. In a group, it is common to create goals that are directed by the person with the most authority. It could be the boss or the parent. It could be the loudest or the smartest voice in the room. When we are connected with our purpose and we resolve what gets in the way, we are better able to share our vision and inspire others in the room. This energy encourages others to share what inspires them. Through sharing inspired ideas, groups can embrace the contrast to develop diverse ideas for more creative solutions.

When we create a supportive space that values the thoughts and ideas of each person involved, each person is engaged to contribute. When we focus on self-care to routinely resolve what bothers us, we are able to get unstuck from our patterned thoughts that others are not listening or that there is a problem if others disagree. We are able to operate as individuals in our groups. Our ideas spark new ideas to create collaborative solutions. We can recognize that when we thrive, those around us are also better able to thrive.

Pillar 4: One simple and powerful model

I have outlined how self-care, a supportive environment, and progress towards goals are important pillars to thrive in our times. This work is made easier when we have a simple and powerful model to support us in resolving our reactions to take meaningful action.

There are many tools and activities to help us thrive. I prefer to use Logosynthesis because it works at a spiritual level. From this level, the work of supporting body and mind can be surprisingly fast and effective. Knowing we are body, mind, and spirit, Willem draws the analogy to a computer. Our body is the hardware. Our mind is the software. Our spirit is the programmer. When we use Logosynthesis, we connect with Essence, our programmer. With this level of connection, we can discover surprising results.

The following overview reminds us why Logosynthesis is an important pillar to support healthy living so that we can thrive in our times:

- We are Essence and we are born with a life purpose.
- Essence is energy in flow and does not suffer.
- When our energy is frozen in painful memories, limiting beliefs, and fantasies, we experience distress.
- Words have the power to restore the flow of energy.
- Logosynthesis provides a guided method to clear what gets in the way of our life purpose.

I recognize that we each have our preferred methods. Our opportunity is to be curious to discover what is possible and to create room for new understanding. When adopting a new approach, it is helpful to remember that it takes time to integrate what we learn. Experiential learning is powerful and we benefit when we share our experiences.

As indicated, the foundation of Logosynthesis is rooted in a core understanding that we are Essence. We do not have to become "more." Others don't have to become "more." We do not aim to change who we are. We simply change how we react to what is. For many, this is a shift from what we have been conditioned to believe. We often think that to be supportive, we need to offer advice. When see each other for who we truly are, as Essence, our perspective shifts. We realize that we each have the power to resolve our distress by resolving the energetic blocks that disconnect us from our Essence. The support that we require is that someone is able to be present, kind, and compassionate. We achieve this by recognizing how we respond to others and doing our own work first.

Using Logosynthesis to restore our flow of energy, we are better able to be present for others. Our opportunity becomes one of resolving our triggers that cause our distress so that we create a space that allows others to connect with their Essence. It may also provide space for them to explore and resolve the triggers to their distress. In many ways, this is the culture that Willem has fostered in the Logosynthesis community. He recognizes that we are all human. We are Essence living in our world, creating our own path forward. He has fostered a community that feels safe for each individual to explore what that means to them individually.

Willem also recognizes the need to maintain the fundamentals of Logosynthesis, given the degree of support that is required to achieve the depth of healing and development. While it appears simple to choose three sentences to shift energy, the method is supported with a very elegant and compassionate theory that allows the sentences to work in a powerful way. The Logosynthesis International Association has been established to protect the quality of training, to certify professionals, and to further develop Logosynthesis. You can refer to the Appendix for more information on LIA.

With this understanding, we can trust the process and begin to apply the technique. We can also learn the theory to help us better understand how it works. We can engage with the Logosynthesis community or a trained guide for additional support. Logosynthesis offers a model that expands our understanding of our human nature. It also offers a fast and easy method to resolve issues that have previously presented as unchangeable.

I recognize that it can be challenging to adopt new models, especially when we have invested heavily in our preferred approach. My upbringing and my corporate training introduced me to concept of 'sunk costs'. This means that the money that has previously been invested in our education or the business has already been spent and should not be a factor in future decisions. In life and in business, there is a need to constantly adapt and innovate to adjust to the changing external environment. The individuals and organizations that are most likely to succeed are those who are able to remain open to new ideas to deliver results. This could require a willingness to walk away from significant investments. I relate this concept because I recognize that for individuals and organizations who have heavily invested in education and training programs, it is very natural to want to continue to improve current programs. As previously mentioned, a survey of professionals trained in Logosynthesis cite these benefits: overall effectiveness; speed of work; ease of use; client comfort and targets the presented issue.

My experience has conditioned me to be open to the benefits of adopting new approaches, even when the transition period can feel uncomfortable or challenging. At times, my conditioning has prompted me to adopt change before the group is ready. When there is resistance in the group, I notice that I react with a thought: Do it anyway. I have been conditioned to jump in and figure things out, even if it feels uncomfortable.

I now recognize this thought as a pattern of reacting. At an anniversary party for my parents, my sister created a video to share their life lessons. Her portion of the video was a fun and interesting clip titled: 'Do it anyway!' In our family, when we were scared or worried about what might happen, we were encouraged to do it anyway. This created lots of interesting adventures and it served us well in life. Yet, I can now observe that at times, our team would have performed better if I had resolved some of the intensity and passion in this thought. My reactions did not always provide the necessary space for others to learn. As we move forward through change and uncertainty, each of us will be influenced by our individual patterns of responding. Taking time to notice our responses allows us to do our own work first to feel more at ease, for ourselves and for others.

I recognize that there are many models to support healthy living. I have based The Healthy Living Plan on Logosynthesis, to offer one simple and powerful model to help us thrive in our times.

Pillar 5: For individuals in groups

We are Essence living in our families, engaging in our workplaces, and interacting in our communities. We each have our own journey. We each experience this journey with others. We live as individuals in social systems. When we remain connected with our Essence, we do not lose our unique identity in our surroundings. We do not need to remove ourselves from our everyday lives. We appreciate the flow of creating with others, even when the conditions are challenging.

As humans, we have a strong desire to feel that we belong to our group. Many people who have moved to a new community can relate to the feeling that even after a number of years, they still feel like outsiders. This is the impact of culture. We may not even be aware of the differences yet subtle variations are woven into what we say and what we do. My parents immigrated to a farm in Canada from the Netherlands. Many aspects of their Western European culture were similar to the dominant Canadian culture in their area, including the color of their skin and their religion. Yet as a family, there were distinct differences from other families in our community. My family farmed in a community known for forestry, fishing, and mining. When I was growing up, I recalled my friends returning to school in the fall and saying they were bored over the summer. We were so busy farming that I could not relate to being bored. These differences in our culture are not better nor worse. They are simply different. Yet when we don't feel like we belong in the group, we can develop reactive patterns of behavior which influence our sense of belonging. As the degree of difference increases, we can experience greater challenges with creating a sense of belonging.

This is also true for other groups, such workplaces and community organizations. Retention and engagement of employees and volunteers depends on people thriving in the culture of the organization. The achievement of collective goals relies on individuals finding their voice in the group. This can present a challenge as we promote diversity in groups. If a different voice is added to a group with lots of similarities, it can be challenging to hear the unique voice. If all voices are different and unique, it can be challenging to find the common ground to hear the collective voice. We begin to shift the culture when we are able to come together from different backgrounds towards a collective goal, while allowing individuals to express their unique contribution.

When our world changes rapidly, our normal patterns and routines no longer feel as comfortable. At times, beliefs and attitudes are so rigid that it prevents acceptance: "That's the way it has always been done." The rigidity of beliefs limits our ability to adapt to our environment and growth is stunted. When Kraft Foods was purchased by Heinz, we were introduced to a new senior management team, made up mainly of Brazilians. There were significant differences in work culture. An example is that in Brazil, it is much more common for working parents to have live-in nannies looking after their children, which allowed parents to work late. In Canada, many working parents juggle work hours and commute times around daycare schedules. The end of their work day in the office is often dictated by the daycare's deadline. This difference in culture resulted in misunderstandings about work commitments and it was a source of anxiety for many employees. In this situation, each person could benefit from using Logosynthesis to resolve their individual triggers, whether the belief that 'employees should work late' or 'I need to leave work on time'. When the triggers are resolved, there will be a greater sense of calm and clarity. Each person will be better able to act on the situation to get the work done, while respecting each individual's situation.

Our society is filled with authoritative messages which can make it challenging to let others be. We adopt this culture of offering advice, which brings an authoritative energy to the group. I noticed this vibe during a workshop. It began with an icebreaker where each person told the group about what was bothering them. A parent was feeling challenged in her relationship with her daughter. A teacher was challenged adjusting to her 'new' job. A woman experienced a challenging interaction at work. There was a lot of advice and support offered by other participants, although this was not part of the exercise. In this workshop setting, the discussion was guided so that each person was able to identify the trigger to what bothered them. The group collectively applied a cycle of Logosynthesis. Each person experienced a unique result. The daughter was ok. 'New' was just a word with no distressing emotions. The response to the interaction was 'Let it go'. In a group dynamic, we often look to offer support by letting others open up about their issues or offering advice but the person is not able to resolve what bothers them. In this case, each person was able to quickly resolve their unique trigger to feel better. Each person in the group felt safe to participate. Participants could recognize the speed and ease of resolving a variety of issues. Logosynthesis provided a structured method to support this safety. Participants were able to feel comfortable to connect with what bothered them to feel relief.

Logosynthesis offers a model to free the energy that is bound in our culture and beliefs. Our everyday interactions will highlight where energy is stuck. We will notice it in the tone of our voice, our eagerness or reluctance to interact, and our how our body responds. The display of emotions will provide cues. The goal is not to change one individual to mold to the group nor to change the group to please one individual. The goal is to use individual reactions as information to break disruptive and limiting patterns. We are better able to tap into the collective creative potential. We are better able to thrive by embracing contrast for a broader perspective and to capture new ideas.

We are Essence. We have a mission in this world. We connect with our unique mission by resolving our triggers. We do not resolve triggers for others. We pay attention to our self-care so we can create a supportive space that inspires others to realize their goals. We are individuals living with others, in our families, our workplaces, and our communities. We are connected. We inspire each other.

Clearing your path for action

Trish North is the Director of Logosynthesis Canada and she has trained and mentored many professionals about the philosophy and application of the model. Trish contributes a beautiful perspective for healing and development, highlighting that Logosynthesis offers a path for discovery. She indicates that the model provides an opportunity to explore what shows up in our lives and to help make sense of things. We receive a great deal of stimulus from our world and this model supports us in taking meaningful action. In this next section, I will describe how you can use the Logosynthesis model to guide your action.

Using the principles of Logosynthesis, you will begin with a focus on what you are here for in your life. Next, you will identify what gets in the way of this purpose and then resolve what bothers you. From a position of greater clarity, you will identify what you need to take action. By resolving your programmed reactions first, you will not be triggered to take action on everything that shows up in your life. You will experience a greater sense of calm and clarity to identify what is meaningful. You will learn to do this routinely as you integrate Logosynthesis into your everyday living. This is not a detailed plan, however. You will learn to trust your intuition and you will be able to adapt as conditions change. You will feel connected to your unique purpose in this life.

In this work, I am often reminded of my mother's advice: "Follow your heart!"

Step 1: Connect with your vision

To discover your path, begin with taking time to explore what inspires you. Notice what brings joy to your life. Notice what is important enough to persevere through challenging times. Notice the moments where you feel connected to what is important and to what has meaning to you personally.

When we develop plans, we often consider vision and purpose from a rational, thinking approach. We are not always tuned in to our inner wisdom and our inner voice. For the purpose of this exercise, you will be guided to connect with your vision and purpose at a higher level of consciousness. Remember that you are exploring your mission in this life. No one else can tell you what this is. For many of us, this may be a new experience. You can approach this as a meditation. The steps are simple:

- Breathe deep and relax.
- Listen for your inner voice and notice what you feel.
- Ask yourself the following questions, allowing about a minute for each question. Jot down any ideas that come to mind, without filtering the responses:

Inspiration:
- What inspires me to be here?
- What inspired me ten years ago?
- What inspired me as a child?

Perspiration:
- What am I willing to work for?
- What was I willing to work for ten years ago?
- What did I love to figure out as a child?

By working back on a timeline, you will notice what has shifted and what has remained constant. You may wish to build on this connection by using drawings or words to illustrate what feels meaningful in the moment. I encourage you not to think about your drawing. Simply capture what comes to mind.

In this exercise, we are looking to connect with the feelings and emotions, rather than a rational response. In the beginning, this may feel slightly uncomfortable and unproductive. We are trained to produce rational responses. When you learn to connect at the level of feeling, you will begin to sense and trust the expression of your Essence.

This work is not to cognitively think about your vision or mission statement. The process is designed to help you feel connected to what you are here for in this life. When you trust your feelings and your inner voice, you will realize that you already have the information.

Step 2: Identify what gets in your way

When we are connected to what inspires us and what we are willing to perspire for in our life, we are able to observe what gets in the way of meaningful action. We can raise our awareness of the barriers. We begin to recognize that the blocks often relate to memories, limiting beliefs, and fantasies. "I am not good enough" and "I should do more" are common beliefs that can get in the way of taking meaningful action. As you take time to become aware of your blocks, you will notice other thoughts, emotions, and physical sensations that hold you back from what is important. This process helps you to recognize the opportunity to clear your path of the frozen perceptions that trigger frozen reactions. You let go of the feeling that you need to change something about yourself or to change the outside world.

I have witnessed many people use Logosynthesis to change frozen perceptions related to being "not good enough". When the images and sounds are gone, they realize they are good enough and feel confident to take action. The type of action I would take when I believe that I am not good enough can be very different from the action that I take when I feel confident in my ability. I experience greater freedom to act in the moment. Therefore, my focus is now to let go of my triggers to patterned reactions so that I can clear my path before I take action.

Here are some ideas to help you identify what gets in your way:

- What thoughts interfere with your aspirations?
- What emotions and body sensations are noticeable when you think about what is important?
- What changes and uncertainties have you experienced that get in the way?
- What issues in your workplace interfere with this vision?
- What things about your relationships hold you back from what is important to you?
- What situations do you avoid?
- What situations make you feel uncomfortable?

Take some time to explore these blocks. Notice the patterns that occur. Connect with the intensity of your reactions. Listen to your self-talk.

Consider that Monica has aspirations to become a vice president in her company. She has worked hard to achieve this goal. Monica identifies a block: her boss, Justin, does not like her. She wants this well-deserved promotion but she feels Justin will not put her name forward. The human resource specialist is good friends with him. Monica is not comfortable bringing the topic of a promotion forward for action. Monica feels rejected and helpless. She begins to tell herself that she doesn't really want the promotion. She begins to look around at other Vice Presidents in the company and she feels that her gender is holding her back. From this position, she is not able to express what she wants. She may rationalize this reaction by changing her goal or quitting her job.

Using her thoughts and emotions as information, Monica can use Logosynthesis to resolve the triggers as they arise. She may notice images of Justin or hear the sound of his voice. After a cycle of Logosynthesis, she may clearly recognize that his response has nothing to do with her and is simply his pattern of reacting. He may in fact, have tremendous respect for her work. She may also notice the feeling relates to an earlier time and the triggers relate to an image of a parent, a schoolmate or a teacher. After a cycle of Logosynthesis, she may notice the feeling is simply gone. In fact, when she resolves her reaction to her boss, their relationship will improve and he will respond differently towards her. Monica's goal is to resolve her triggers, rather than to change others or the organization. However, with time, as she gains a sense of clarity and confidence, her actions can influence meaningful change.

Taking time to identify barriers within yourself allows you to know what blocks to resolve before you take action. When you acknowledge that frozen perceptions trigger frozen reactions, it is easier to be aware of the blocks. You can then use Logosynthesis to resolve what bothers you.

Step 3: Resolve what bothers you

When we feel connected to our mission and we have clarity about what gets in the way, we can resolve the triggers that block our path. This work uses the Logosynthesis method, as outlined in Chapter 3. You are not looking to resolve all the blocks at once. Your aim is simply to begin to restore the flow of your creative energy and shift from reaction to action.

You can create your list based on the blocks that were identified in Step 2 above. Write down each issue. Decide which block you would like to resolve first. Follow the Logosynthesis method to resolve the trigger. Take your time and when ready, decide on the next issue you wish to resolve.

Be gentle as you approach this work. Some patterns of response have helped you to get by in life for a long time. You may require support to let go of these frozen patterns. You may feel that if you let go, you will not be able to fight or power forward on important issues. I encourage you to simply trust the process. You are accessing your Essence. When you restore the flow of your energy, it will be available to support you with your mission in this life.

At times, you may notice very strong reactions when the energy shifts. In these cases, allow more time for the sentences to process. Be easy on yourself and reach out for support from trained professionals (refer to resources in the Appendix). This is an investment to help you move beyond your reactions and distress to take action. In the beginning, this may not feel comfortable but as you learn to trust the process, you will realize that you only need to connect with the distressing sensations for a short period of time to let go. You will learn to appreciate the grace and flow of the work. You will understand that you are Essence.

It is important to resolve what bothers you before taking action. If you create an action plan when you are feeling a lot of resistance, the work will be much harder and less effective. For example, Mark is managing an important project, under a tight deadline, with Maria, Sue, and Carlos. Sue and Carlos have very different ideas about what needs to be done. Mark has worked hard to change their minds because he knows that he is right. He feels that because he is the boss, they should listen to him. He feels that they are getting in the way of the work of the team. If Mark takes action without resolving what bothers him, his action will reflect that Sue and Carlos are the issue. He reprimands them in front of their peers, contacts Human Resources to complain or works hard to hold back his words. This creates feelings of tension in the relationships and, ironically, prevents work from getting done.

Mark takes time to apply Logosynthesis. He connects with his thoughts, emotions and body sensations. He recognizes the thought: "I am the boss and they should listen to me." He is frustrated and angry and notices that he is clenching his jaw. He connects with the level of distress. He hears the voice of a previous boss and he identifies the trigger as "the sound of my boss saying these words". As the sentences process, he feels calmer and he clearly recognizes that he also has to listen to his employees. Sue and Carlos notice that he is more open to listening to their points of concern. When they feel heard rather than challenged, they are better able to express their concerns calmly. Mark is made aware of a blind spot that could have derailed the project. The improved relationship allows the team to proactively adjust their plan for a more successful outcome.

When our distressing thoughts and emotions are resolved, disruptive patterns of behavior fall away. Each person in the group benefits from resolving their unique triggers. While it is common to look to what others should do differently, I now focus on doing my own work to create a more supportive environment. When Mark, Maria, Sue, and Carlos each take responsibility to resolve their own reactions, the team feels better able to handle contrasting ideas and engaged to fully participate. The team is in a better position to successfully complete the important project, while maintaining relationships.

Step 4: Take action

Taking action is key to realizing your mission in this world. We are Essence, born with a mission in this life. As we

Integrating Logosynthesis into everyday living

access Essence, we experience more flow to allow us to thrive in our everyday lives. When we are aware of what we are here for in this life, we are better able to identify what gets in the way and resolve what bothers us. When triggers no longer dictate our distressing automatic responses, we can choose to act rather than feel controlled by frozen reactions. We feel safe and supported to participate in our families, workplaces, and communities.

I remember my first full-time job. I was one of two employees hired for a new role in quality assurance. The conditions on the production floor felt intense. Being an engineer would have been a strong asset to better understand the operation. The unionized employees didn't readily trust that we were checking their work. The quality assurance office was a much calmer place to spend time than out on the floor with the employees. However, I realized that if I was to learn, I had to be on the production floor to experience what was happening. I had to understand how the equipment operated and I had to understand how the team operated. I knew that reading quality assurance manuals were important but that the action was on the production floor. I realized that I could not do my job if I was not engaged in what was happening around me. I needed to interact with others to access resources and to learn. I needed to resolve my resistance to the idea that the employees did not want me checking on them and take action to do my job well. In retrospect, I believe I could have better managed my role with fewer curse words and more ease if I had access to Logosynthesis at the time.

After we resolve what blocks our way, our energy is available to take action. The following questions will guide the process:

- What resources do I need?
- What do I need to learn?
- What barriers I will encounter?
- Who can help me?
- What is my timeline?
- What are my key actions now?

When we are clear of the energetic blocks, we have more clarity of the path forward. This is not a static plan because as we gain experiences and as our world changes, we can adapt. Yet we may be surprised how the actions fall into place. We will recognize the flow of extraordinary living.

Step 5: Get in the flow

I am human. I get triggered. I react in situations. I react to the world around me based on my life experiences, my cultural attitudes, and my interesting beliefs. Triggers will continue to influence how I respond. I am now more aware of my responses and how to resolve unwanted patterns. I also am more aware of the impact of my responses on others in my family, my workplace, and my community.

Something magical happens when I recognize that my automatic responses are actually frozen reaction patterns which are triggered by frozen perceptions. I now know that I have the power to shift these patterns. I can now resolve unwanted or distressing patterns to adapt to change and uncertainty in our times. This is powerful!

When I am no longer resisting change, I feel calmer. My responses feel more respectful to others. I can respond to the world as it is, not how I believe it should be or how I wish it was. I can support my groups by contributing to a culture of respect. I know that when others feel safe, they are better able to contribute toward shared goals. I know from a position of leadership, that my actions have a strong influence on the overall culture of the group. I am better able to hold the space to feel safe and supportive for others. When roles and expectations are not clear, we experience tension. When we remain calm while others are triggered, we can help them to feel calmer. When we collectively realize the benefit of calming our reactions, the culture of the group shifts to access more of our creative energy.

During times of change and uncertainty, it is easy to get stuck in reminiscing about our past or wishing for the future. When we experience sudden change, loss, and uncertainty, we freeze our energy in perceptions of the exceptional events. We also reactivate triggers of distressing events from our past. It is easy to become stuck in thinking about what could have or should have happened.

It may not be easy to acknowledge our current situation because it is uncomfortable or painful. We may push these feelings aside and focus on other things. We may work harder. We may avoid the situation all together. We develop coping strategies so that we feel better in the moment, yet over time things may become dysfunctional.

Logosynthesis provides me with a model to accept my circumstances. I have confidence that when I connect with what bothers me, I am able to follow a simple method that will help me feel better. The more comfortable I get with using the method, the more confident I am that I can use the power of three specific sentences to relieve distressing thoughts, emotions, and body sensations. I also have a better understanding of what bothers me and of how those around me are responding.

Logosynthesis is certainly not the only resource to help me feel better. I enjoy nature, music, exercise, prayer, connecting with others, and focusing on meaningful projects. However, Logosynthesis helps me better understand why these approaches that support an energetic connection are helpful and important.

As you discover your path, you will realize your power to guide the process of adapting to the world in which we live. You become better able to focus on what is important in changing and uncertain circumstances. This is a dynamic process. If we connect with what is important and identify what gets in the way at a cognitive level, we may think that we need to change external factors in our life. When we connect at an energetic level and we take time to resolve the triggers, we have more clarity to take action. We may think that individuals are blocks to what we want to achieve, yet, through this process, we may realize that they provide valuable resources to support our mission.

An illustrated guide

This section provides illustrations to guide your work. I recommend that you review your vision on an annual basis. You can create routines to identify what gets in the way, resolve the blocks, and take action on a more regular basis. When our energy is flowing, rather than stuck in frozen patterns, we can trust our intuition.

As this process becomes routine, you will have the ability to quickly notice your resistance and let it go. You will also notice increased feelings of peace and compassion, which will help to both improve your relationships and offer support to others.

In the beginning, this process may feel quite private to you. You may feel that there are many things that stand in the way of what is important. As you continue to resolve what bothers you, you will feel more comfortable in sharing these thoughts with others. When others know what is meaningful to you, they are better able to offer support. You may feel resistance to the people who can provide resources. As you gradually release this resistance, you will feel the support of others. You will have the increased satisfaction of creating with others. This is the beauty of using Logosynthesis: to shift from reacting to the world around us to creating in this world with others.

Restoring the flow of our energy is a process. For some, energy may be stuck in outward, angry reactions. Others may experience more inward reactions of shame and guilt. As you resolve these blocks, you may experience more angry reactions. This outward expression may feel uncomfortable to others. When we understand that this response is a reaction to a trigger, we are better able to hold space and feel calm. As triggers are resolved, the energy continues to shift from anger towards kindness and compassion. Actions, reactions, and interactions continue to shift toward more meaningful action.

Remembering that our automatic responses can feel more intense during change and uncertainty is helpful. In my position in sales, it was common to be assigned aggressive targets and to be offered bonuses for achieving these targets. The financial reward was even more substantial for senior management. There was significant motivation to 'hit the number'. In ordinary times, we knew what we had to do and how to do it. When the company was purchased, suddenly we no longer felt comfortable about expectations.

Integrating Logosynthesis into everyday living

The targets were more aggressive. The bonus was bigger. Our team was different. We were more easily triggered and our work felt more intense.

I used Logosynthesis to help me focus. The urge to contribute to repetitive discussions about what "could" and "should" happen fell away. I was better able to voice my concerns with less intensity. I was able to achieve my targets. My coworkers noticed the shift. We actually had some fun noticing when I got triggered. I used their feedback to help me recognize what bothered me. I was better able to avoid getting stuck in reactive patterns and to simply do what was being asked of me.

We are all human. We all react. We all have the power to influence the world around us in a more positive way. I love how the following quote flows with the work of Logosynthesis!

> *We keep moving forward, opening new doors, and doing new things, because we're curious and curiosity keeps leading us down new paths.*
>
> — Walt Disney —

There can be a lot of reactions connected to opening new doors: limiting beliefs, voices of authority, memories of past experiences, and fantasies about what could happen. When we free this energy, we are in a position to explore new paths and create something meaningful. We are able to take action to clear our own path!

I remember attending my first Logosynthesis training seminar in April 2015. My life was extremely busy. I certainly did not have time to dedicate a weekend to attend a seminar. Yet I felt that it was important to be there. I had a strong awareness that this work was profound. I recognized that Logosynthesis was an extraordinary model that could guide me and others through challenging times. I remember coming home and telling David that I was blown away with what I learned. From that point forward, I embraced the opportunity to share what I was learning. I knew that people, like me, were often unaware of how their patterns of reacting created issues for themselves and those around them. Like me, they believed that Logosynthesis could benefit their friends, coworkers and family members. We did not feel that we were the ones that needed to change. I had begun to realize the power of simply focusing on my own reactions and noticing how my life shifted for the better. I had begun to experience the joy of having my energy in flow to embrace extraordinary living.

Integrating Logosynthesis into everyday living

The Vision
CONNECT WITH WHAT IS MEANINGFUL.

INSPIRATION

what inspires me now?

what inspired me 10 years ago?

what inspired me as a child?

PERSPIRATION

what am i willing to work for now?

what was i willing to work for 10 years ago?

what did i love to figure out as a child?

draw what feels meaningful in the moment:

The blocks
IDENTIFY WHAT GETS IN THE WAY.

make some notes about what gets in the way:

thoughts →

feelings →

work →

other people →

what i need →

Integrating Logosynthesis into everyday living

The Triggers
LET GO OF WHAT BOTHERS YOU.

create a list of things that bother you:

- ☐ _____
- ☐ _____
- ☐ _____
- ☐ _____

decide which you would like to resolve first.

use Logosynthesis for each item.

THE ACTION
DESIGN YOUR ACTION MAP.

plan your action:

WHAT RESOURCES DO I NEED?

WHAT DO I NEED TO LEARN?

WHO CAN HELP ME?

WHAT IS MY TIMELINE?

WHAT ARE MY KEY ACTIONS NOW?

the flow

ENJOY EXTRAORDINARY LIVING!

keep your plan top of mind and let it flow!

REVIEW the vision ANNUALLY.

BE AWARE OF the blocks AS YOU MOVE FORWARD.

RESOLVE the triggers ROUTINELY - DAILY OR WEEKLY. AS NEEDED

UPDATE the action AS YOU GET NEW INFORMATION.

Having impact in our groups

I have described how our reactions can interfere with taking meaningful action and I have showed you how to use Logosynthesis to connect with what is meaningful in your life. It doesn't matter where you are now in your life. You can use your everyday reactions as information to tap into your creative energy. This is not always easy and you will benefit from the support of a trained professional. As you move beyond reactive patterns of behavior, you will be in a position to have a more positive impact with your family, your workplace, and your community.

When considering your individual impact in your groups, it is helpful to remember that each of us:

- is Essence
- has a life purpose
- lives this purpose in our world
- will face challenges and opportunities
- has an opportunity to resolve our distress
- has an opportunity to make an impact

Our work is not to change others. Our work is to restore the flow of our life energy, which will create a space that feels more supportive for others. When we are able to connect with others respectfully, we can better influence changes in the world around us. With an appreciation that each of us is Essence, born with a life purpose, the following overview will help you consider your interactions with others.

Our family

In families, each person has a role. The role of the parent is to teach values, to set boundaries, and provide children with a safe and supportive space to learn and to grow. The role of the parent is to prepare the child to venture out on their own. The role of the child is to explore the world within the safety and boundaries of the family. The child learns the culture and explores new opportunities. Grandparents, aunts, uncles, and cousins help to establish the culture and traditions of the family within the community.

The values of the family are based on the culture and beliefs of the parents, within the context their community in their time. Boundaries will be enforced based on cultural and societal norms. The safety that a child feels will be influenced by the degree of safety that is experienced by their parent.

The world changes. As children grow, they have experiences beyond their family. The new experiences may collide with the familiar norms. This contrast can lead to tension in relationships. Children react to their parents and vice versa. Through experience, new norms are adopted. When our world suddenly changes, we feel more tension due to uncertainty. During the pandemic, parents lost jobs, children could not attend school, and grandparents could not visit. Each individual had a unique experience in the context of their family. How each person reacted influenced the response of others. Patterns were formed. These patterns influenced the experience of each individual in the family.

For example, a father may have lost his job during the pandemic. His frozen perception may be tied to the belief that a father should provide for his family. His frozen reaction to this trigger may be an angry outburst. In everyday situations, he may feel triggered when he is reminded that he does not have a job. The mother and children do not feel safe or supported in this environment. With an understanding of Logosynthesis, each person can use their own reactions as information to shift how they feel so they can calm reactive patterns. It can be expected that the greatest impact will be if the father does his work to resolve his angry outbursts. When the father feels calm, despite having lost his job, his wife and children are better able to feel calm.

When individuals within the family are aware of their reactions, the rigid patterns can begin to shift. When individuals know that they can get help to resolve the intensity of feelings, this can support healing. It is the role of the parents to create a level of support and safety for their children. Some individuals will require more time, space, and compassion than others to resolve what bothers them.

When we have an awareness of the process, we can collectively commit to doing our own work. We feel calmer and we are better able to be compassionate with and supportive to others.

Our workplace

We primarily join workplaces to earn income to meet our financial goals. We also desire to feel that our work is meaningful. Regardless of our role in the organization, we react to the demands of our workplace based on habitual responses. When external conditions are rapidly changing and uncertain, we may feel anxious or overwhelmed. We respond to our environment based on our values, beliefs, and attitudes but our personal reactions will impact our group.

Many workplaces are governed by a Board of Directors and led by a senior management team. Their influence is felt throughout the organization. When Board members and senior management have an awareness of their triggers and commit to changing their frozen reactions at an individual level, the results will benefit the entire organization. When the work of changing frozen reactions begins at the Board level, it creates an open, trusting atmosphere to embrace change and uncertainty. This supports the culture of the entire organization. Senior management are better able to create a space that feels safe for employees to fully participate in their work. This engaging space supports individuals in making progress towards goals and reduces the symptoms of burnout, absenteeism, and conflict. When those in senior positions know how to resolve what bothers them, they can provide a stronger sense of support for their teams, even when circumstances are challenging.

The corporate mission statement provides the direction for the entire organization. A company aims to earn the hearts and souls of its employees and its customers. It is powerful to support employees to connect with this mission statement at an energetic rather than at a cognitive level. Each person will be able to recognize what stands in the way of this vision for them personally.

When Kraft Heinz was formed in 2015, the vision was communicated: *To be the best food company, growing a better world*. I loved it! Based on my background in agriculture and training as a dietitian, I felt inspired. As we moved forward, it became clear that individuals had different ideas of what this looked like for a leading, multinational food company. I was frustrated when some of the new product launches did not align with my interpretation of being the 'best food company'. There were so many opinions linked to the words "best" and "better." For some, it meant solely to be the most profitable food company. For others, it meant to have the most nutritious products. Still others had passion for sustainability and social responsibility. Sharing stories of what was being done to be the 'best', such as having employees participate in their humanitarian, micronutrient campaign, helped everyone focus on a shared vision.

When we look to make an impact in our workplace, we can focus on our individual reactions and actions. When we shift the energy stuck in habitual patterns, we are better able to focus on our work, have better conversations, and create an engaging work environment. When we operate collectively, we shift the culture, beliefs, and attitudes of the entire organization. In times of change and uncertainty, this is the work that embraces diversity to support the workplace and allow everyone to thrive.

Our community

Our community involves many groups, including schools and volunteer organizations. Each of us contributes to what makes our community feel unique. This is a space that can provide significant safety and support to its members. It can also be a space that limits growth and opportunity.

Schools are structured to provide a safe space for students to study new information, share experiences, and develop relationships that support learning and development. The teachers and professors create safety and engagement in the learning experience. The administration enforces the rules so the space is safe and supportive. However, students arrive at school with different capacities to learn. Based on experiences outside of school, students may engage in behaviors that reduce the level of safety and support in the group. The behaviors of students can influence whether other students are able to learn. Whether you are a student, a teacher, or an administrator, you have an opportunity to resolve your reactions to create a meaningful learning experience, for yourself and those around you.

When teachers are frustrated, overwhelmed, or disengaged, students perceive this energy. The learning experience is negatively impacted and students suffer. When students are disengaged, this negatively influences the teachers' experiences. A pattern is formed. While each teacher and student can resolve what bothers them to shift this pattern, the work is enhanced when the administrative leaders also engage in the work at their level. Often times, when leaders do their own work first, the level of support and safety felt throughout the organization reduces the reactive behaviors of the group. There is a reduced need for everyone to do their own work because they already feel safe and supported.

Non-profit and volunteer organizations also play an important role in our communities. By their nature, there is a sense of common purpose. Individual experiences, values, and beliefs will influence contribution. At times, individual passions will get in the way of achieving the collective vision. A common frustration of people supporting community groups is that they have difficulty agreeing on the action required to achieve these goals. In these situations, it can be valuable to review the vision, individually identify the blocks, and resolve what gets in the way. This allows individuals to resolve the energy bound in their beliefs to better work toward the shared vision.

We have impact in our groups when we have a clear vision of our purpose, when we can identify what gets in our way, and when we resolve what bothers us. We can take meaningful action to create what we desire, as individuals in our groups. When our world is rapidly changing, our vision may remain the same but there is an increased need to be aware of what gets in the way of achieving our vision. Logosynthesis offers a method to resolve what gets in the way so our creative energy is available to focus on our vision. We will take action from a position of clarity.

Our world can suddenly change and Logosynthesis can help calm our reactions to support meaningful action. We have an opportunity to commit to this journey and to thrive in our times!

Conclusion

When our energy is frozen, there is resistance.
There is no flow.
We get stuck in trying to control the outcome.
Letting go is about opening up to possibility and opportunity.

We enjoy healthy living when we feel well: physically, mentally, and emotionally. We enjoy extraordinary living when we are able to move beyond our normal routines and we feel connected to our unique mission in life. As we learn to use our reactions as information to resolve what gets in the way, we create space for meaningful action. We have an opportunity to realize the amazing power that we have within ourselves. We are more than body and mind. We are Essence. Our words have power to restore the flow of our creative energy to support our mission in this life.

Logosynthesis helps us to notice how our body and mind respond in our everyday experiences, even during difficult times. We can pay attention to what bothers us and resolve the frozen perceptions that trigger frozen reactions. We feel more peace and calm to support our health and to support others. We feel more kindness and compassion to create a positive influence in our world. We are better able to influence rather than force others in our changing and uncertain world.

Personally, I am more committed than ever to resolving

my triggers to enjoy life and to help others. After many years of busy routines at home, at work, and in my community, I use Logosynthesis to help me shift from what is urgent to what is important in my life. I now feel more comfortable sharing my experiences to help others realize their power. When I inevitably encounter blocks along my path, I know how to resolve them to feel more confident about the next steps.

I know the world will continue to change and that events in my life will feel uncertain and challenging. Events may impact me individually, such as illness or loss. They may also be broader in scope, such as a pandemic, social movements, or climate change. I experienced the events of the global pandemic as an individual and as part of our global community. I know that our children will remember how they felt from both their own experience and from the responses of those around them. They will pass along these feelings, in some form, to their children. I do my work first to feel peace and calm so that our children can enjoy a sense of safety in their surroundings.

I am now more aware of my reactions and how they impact others. Casual remarks that may have previously passed as acceptable behavior in my circle of friends, may now be a trigger for some people. I now know why others respond differently from me. I also know how to resolve what bothers me to create a more supportive space. I am better able to embrace extraordinary living during extraordinary times.

Conclusion

EXTRAORDINARY *times* call for EXTRAORDINARY *living*

I commit to this journey with a focus on self-care. I will not be successful in preventing reactive behavior in each instance. However, I now have a greater appreciation for how to resolve my reactive patterns. When I use my reactions as information, I can shift my energy for increased calm, clarity, and focus.

I commit to this journey with a focus on creating a supportive environment. Owning and resolving my individual reactions creates space for others to feel safe. When I do my individual work, I notice a shift. I feel better. I am able to act, think, and make better choices. As I use the method regularly, I soften my rigid, limiting beliefs so that I can create better dialogue. In the process, something beautiful happens. My energy can inspire and influence others.

I commit to the journey with a focus on progressing towards my goals. I am inspired by a vision of what is possible in my life, in my community, and in my world. I am better able to collaborate with others to realize a shared vision and to take action to support our shared values.

I commit to the journey using one simple and powerful model. I know that my spirit is the operator of my body and my mind. When I operate from Essence in this world, I am free to act. I am able to trust Logosynthesis to guide my journey because I know that it has been developed from a deep understanding of the power of Essence for healing and development. I know the sentences have been specifically crafted with Willem's knowledge, experience, and intuition. I know the method allows me to restore the flow of my creative energy, even if I don't know how it happens. I am better able to adapt rather than getting stuck in my memories, limiting beliefs, and fantasies about how life should be.

I commit to the journey knowing that I am an individual, living with others. Together, we create through our families, our workplaces, and our communities. Our groups contain powerful energy fields, which help us feel comfortable when we operate according to our group norms. These energy fields can also trigger uncomfortable responses when conditions change. I receive information and feedback to keep me connected to my groups. I also can access

Conclusion

my power to learn, heal, and grow beyond the limitations of my groups.

As I clear my path using Logosynthesis, I feel inspired. I am not sure where my path will lead but I trust the journey. As I wrote this book during the turbulence of the pandemic, I enjoyed the luxury of a very creative space right at home on the lake. I felt connected with my family and, remotely, with a very supportive community.

This book has described how you can use Logosynthesis to resolve what bothers you to clear your path for your mission in life. It can help you access your wonderful human potential. When you restore the flow of your Essence to achieve peace and meaning in your life, you will contribute to healing our collective challenges. Your energy will contribute to feelings of kindness and compassion in our world. You will experience the flow of extraordinary living.

Change can inspire excitement, creativity, and compassion. We can experience rapid shifts in areas of our life where we previously felt stuck. Each of us is extraordinary! We each hold a special talent to offer the world. Something unique that no one else can express. We each have the opportunity to go beyond our norms to express our unique talent. I encourage you to use this book as a guide to help shift your reactions to take meaningful action to thrive in our times. Enjoy!

Appendix

Glossary of terms in Logosynthesis®

The terms used in the book are standard terms used in Logosynthesis and defined by Willem Lammers in *Sparks at Dawn: Awakening with Logosynthesis®. Reflections on the Journey. (Logosynthesis Live Book 3)* as follows:

Belief, limiting belief:
A (limiting) belief hinders one's self-perception and available options in the current environment. It also hinders the unfolding of one's potential. A (limiting) belief can be acquired from important primary relationships or it can be a conclusion that is reached in reaction to statements made or behaviors demonstrated by these important people.

Cycle:
A sequence of three Logosynthesis sentences with their working pauses. A reflection phase follows a cycle, allowing the processed aspect to be integrated into the client's frame of reference. A session will sometimes contain only one cycle or even no cycles at all, but sessions with between five and seven cycles are not uncommon.

Emotions:
Emotions are innate elements of human experience that are directly tied to an individual's perception of their environment and their corresponding accommodation behaviors

(e.g., surprise, joy, rage, fear, revulsion, grief). Emotions serve the survival of individuals and social systems by supporting decision-making, the development of values and norms, and the finding of adequate behaviors for interaction with the environment.

Healthy emotions relate to other people or events in the present. Archaic emotions are frozen reactions to people or events in the past. Logosynthesis acts to identify archaic emotions and dissolve them, allowing individuals to react with healthy emotions.

Energy Structure:

The flow of energy can be influenced by distressing events and then frozen in structures. These structures contain perceptions that are stored in an individual's body and personal space. The structures also contain physical, emotional, and cognitive reactions to the perceptions.

Essence:

A human being is a manifestation of a comprehensive Essence that exists beyond time and space. Religious and spiritual traditions call Essence the higher Self, the true Self, or the immortal soul. Logosynthesis borrows the term *Essence* from Ali Hameed Almaas and uses it as a neutral concept to avoid associations with existing religions, spiritual paths, or schools of guided change. Essence manifests as a Self with a body and psyche in the Earth Life System.

Appendix

Fantasy:

A fantasy is an idea about how the world is, how it could/should be, or how it could/should have been. It is distinguished from sensory perceptions and memories, both of which represent the world in the past or present with the help of the senses. Fantasies are generally just as important as sensory perceptions and memories. The reality content of fantasies varies: a plan may include concrete steps to bring about its realization, while a wish or dream delegates the realization to other people or elements of the outside world.

Feeling:

A feeling can denote an emotion, a fantasy, an intuition, a physical sensation, a kinesthetic perception, a thought, a hypothesis, or a belief. Clarification is always required when this word is used in Logosynthesis, as different meaning can lead to different interventions.

Frozen Perception:

A frozen perception occurs when sensory experiences of a memory are frozen into an energetic structure. Frozen perceptions are inseparably linked to frozen reactions.

Frozen Reaction:

A frozen reaction includes physical, emotional, cognitive, and behavioral aspects. Frozen reactions are always connected to a trigger. The same reactions will always occur if the associated trigger is activated. Logosynthesis is only concerned with reactions that directly or indirectly lead to suffering.

Life Energy:
Life energy is the power of growth within nature that causes organisms to develop into higher forms, embryos to become adults, and healthy people to strive after their ideals. This power has different names in various cultures, including ka, physis, prana, chi, the zero-point field, and, in this book, Essence. Life energy can be flowing or frozen and can belong to an individual or to people and objects within an individual's environment.

Personal Space:
An individual's personal space is a portion of the three-dimensional field in the Earth Life System that the individual experiences as their own. Personal space usually contains the individual's physical body as well as introjects and dissociated parts. Personal space can equally be understood as an extended aura or an energy field.

Processing:
The Logosynthesis sentences have been developed for and are addressed to elements of experience such as memories and fantasies. The saying of each sentence is followed by

a working pause in which the power of words neutralizes or assimilates the targeted element. Once a sentence's processing is complete, the emotional charge of the targeted element is reduced or has disappeared. The individual can then gauge the experience from an age-appropriate perspective.

Representation:
A representation, or image, is a three-dimensional energy structure in space that is formed of frozen sensory perceptions (i.e. sight, hearing, touch, smell, taste.) It can depict a memory, fantasy, or belief. Representations (or images) must be assimilated to become functional.

Self:
The Self is a specific manifestation of Essence within the context of the Earth Life System. The Self controls a body with which it perceives the environment and navigates space, along with a brain that processes information from the sensory organs. It also controls a psyche that directs the body and brain in their confrontations with the environment.

Parts of the energy of the Self can be split off, frozen, or dissociated. The part of the Self in which a person's life energy is flowing freely is called the Real Self or the Free Self.

Trigger:
A trigger is an introject that is activated by people or events in an individual's current environment. Triggers take the form of frozen perceptions and inevitably lead to predictable physical, emotional, and cognitive reactions.

Working Pause:
The time taken after each Logosynthesis sentence to process the information that has been given to your system. In this pause, different reactions are possible from yawning and relaxation to deep emotions.

Appendix

Books on Logosynthesis®

Lammers, Willem (2015). *Self-Coaching with Logosynthesis®.* Also available in German, Serbian and Italian.

Lammers, Willem (2015). *Logosynthesis® Handbook for the Helping Professions.* Also in German and Dutch.

Lammers, Willem (2019). *Minute Miracles. The Practice of Logosynthesis®. Inspiration from Real Life.* Also available in German.

Lammers, Willem (2020). *Reclaiming Your Energy from Your Emotions. States of the Mind in Logosynthesis®. See Your Self, Be Your Self.* Also available in German.

Lammers, Willem (2020). *Sparks at Dawn. Awakening with Logosynthesis®. Reflections on the Journey.*

Lammers, Willem (2020). *Discover Logosynthesis®: The Power of Words in Healing and Development.*

Caswell, Cathy (2017). *Logosynthesis®: Enjoying Life More Fully: Recharge. Revitalize. Reconnect.*

Weiss, Laurie (2016). *Letting It Go: Relieve Anxiety and Toxic Stress in Just a Few Minutes Using Only Words. Rapid Relief with Logosynthesis®.* Also in German.

Weiss, Laurie & Lammers, Willem (2020). *Embrace Prosperity. Resolve Blocks to Experiencing Abundance. Rapid Relief with Logosynthesis®.*

Additional Resources on Logosynthesis®

To find a certified coach, counselor or therapist:
http://www.logosynthesis.international/professionals

Logosynthesis International Association (LIA):
LIA is an independent, international non-profit organization based in Switzerland. The LIA:

- Supports professionals and other interested parties with Logosynthesis.
- Establishes a worldwide Logosynthesis network with numerous active hubs.
- Offers a platform for the exchange of knowledge and experience.
- Contributes to the spread of Logosynthesis.
- Promotes the quality and further development of Logosynthesis.
- Certifies professionals across various levels

Practitioners and Master Practitioners in Logosynthesis® are trained specialists from counseling, educational, and medical professions.

The Logosynthesis International Association provides a wealth of information for those who want to know more, especially for people seeking support and for professionals who want to be certified.

Appendix

Logosynthesis International Association
Website: www.logosynthesis.international
Email: contact@logosynthesis.international

Willem Lammers | The Origin of Logosynthesis®
Website: www.logosynthesis.net
Contact: info@logosynthesis.net
Facebook: www.facebook.com/groups/logosynthesis
YouTube: The Origin of Logosynthesis

The Healthy Living Plan®
Website: www.thehealthylivingplan.com
Contact: info@thehealthylivingplan.com
Facebook: www.facebook.com/thehealthylivingp
YouTube: The Healthy Living Plan

Cathy Caswell - Author
Website: www.cathycaswell.com
Contact: info@cathycaswell.com
Facebook: www.facebook.com/CathyCaswellAuthor
YouTube: Cathy Caswell

About the Author

Cathy Caswell is the president of The Healthy Living Plan Inc. and the author of *Logosynthesis: Enjoying Life More Fully*. She recognizes the inspiring power of creating with those around us. Her interest in Logosynthesis as a model for healing and development is driven by a passion to support individuals to thrive in their families, workplaces, and communities.

This book is based on the author's personal experience using Logosynthesis in her everyday life, including times of change and uncertainty: *'As I reflect on my life choices, I can now observe that my patterns of behavior are based on my beliefs, attitudes, and experiences. These patterns have served me well. Work hard. Help others. Stick with it. Yet I can also observe where these patterns have become rigid and overused. When I experience change and uncertainty and my energy is stuck in these patterns, it can be difficult to see other ways of doing things. My automatic responses can feel intense and distressing, for myself and for those around me. Logosynthesis allows me to clear my path to move forward with greater ease and clarity.'*

As a certified Practitioner and Instructor in Logosynthesis®, she uses the method for her own professional self-care, to coach others and to teach the method for self-coaching. She shares her knowledge and personal experience to help others understand and appreciate the benefits of using Logosynthesis to thrive in our times.

www.ingramcontent.com/pod-product-compliance
Lightning Source LLC
Chambersburg PA
CBHW070421010526
44118CB00014B/1846